A Clear Water Stream

Other books by Henry Williamson

The Flax of Dream, the story
of Willie Maddison,
comprising four separate
volumes:

THE BEAUTIFUL YEARS
DANDELION DAYS
THE DREAM OF FAIR WOMEN
THE PATHWAY
(Faber and Faber)

*A Chronicle of Ancient
Sunlight:*

THE DARK LANTERN
DONKEY BOY
YOUNG PHILLIP MADDISON
HOW DEAR IS LIFE
A FOX UNDER MY CLOAK
THE GOLDEN VIRGIN
LOVE AND THE LOVELESS
A TEST TO DESTRUCTION
THE INNOCENT MOON
IT WAS THE NIGHTINGALE
THE POWER OF THE DEAD
THE PHOENIX GENERATION
A SOLITARY WAR
LUCIFER BEFORE SUNRISE
THE GALE OF THE WORLD
(Macdonald and Jane's)

Other Novels

THE STAR-BORN
THE GOLD FALCON
(Faber and Faber)

Country Books

LIFE IN A DEVON VILLAGE
TALES OF A DEVON VILLAGE
SALAR THE SALMON
THE PHASIAN BIRD
THE STORY OF A NORFOLK FARM
SCRIBBLING LARK
(Faber and Faber)

Nature Books

THE LONE SWALLOWS
THE PEREGRINE'S SAGA,
   and other Wild Tales
THE OLD STAG,
   and other Hunting Stories
TARKA THE OTTER
(The Bodley Head)
TALES OF MOORLAND AND
   ESTUARY
THE HENRY WILLIAMSON
   ANIMAL SAGA
COLLECTED NATURE STORIES
THE SCANDAROON
(Macdonald and Jane's)

A Clear Water Stream

Henry Williamson

Illustrations by Peter Cross

MACDONALD AND JANE'S · LONDON

First published in 1958 by
Faber and Faber Limited

This new revised, illustrated edition published in 1975 by
Macdonald and Jane's
(Macdonald & Co. (Publishers) Ltd),
Paulton House, 8 Shepherdess Walk, London N1

Copyright in text © Henry Williamson, 1958, 1975
Copyright in illustrations © Macdonald and Jane's, 1975

ISBN 0 356 08202 4

Printed and bound in Great Britain by
REDWOOD BURN LIMITED
Trowbridge & Esher

To Loetitia who said,
'Thank you for giving me
such beautiful children.'

Contents

Fishing Cottage

We had decided to move at Michaelmas; and some time before quarter day we went to look at a small house in a valley below the moor. An advertisement in the local paper said that two miles of fishing were to be let with the place. A trout stream! I had not fished since before the war. Those days of boyhood seemed ended for ever: could I take it up again, would I feel the same?

Our first visit to the cottage was made in summer weather. We stopped at a bridge over the river, seeing thatched roofs through the leaves of tall beech trees. Around us were the pastures of a deer park, the cooing of wild pigeons, the distant *jacks* of daws, the humming of bees, the echo of running water. Looking over the stone parapet of the bridge, I saw the stream running clear over gravel. It was illumined by sun below one bank. The water flowing past a large tree on the opposite bank was deep, moving slowly: and as I stared down, into depths that had the bloom of a grape, it seemed that a tail was slowly idling by the roots. This was exciting; and as 'our' fishing ended at the bridge, we climbed the tarred railings on the opposite side of the lane, and descending by a vertical ladder fixed below the bank, walked forward on the grass, into sunshine, and the open space of the park. This was the place to live, we told one another, as we stood upon an ornamental bridge rising steeply upon three arches.

Below the bridge was a deep and wide pool, fed by three streams cascading under the arches. The pool shelved, and broke into innumerable murmuring rills over shallows lying between grassy banks. There was a break in the turf made by the feet of cattle and horses, which had gone there to drink, and cross. Was this the ford, which gave the hamlet its name?

Standing on the ornamental bridge of grey igneous rock, I looked into clear water upstream. There lay, sleepily, several trout, their hues varying with the colours beneath them: dark brown of back where they rested upon water-moss growing on rock-layers; brown over beds of gravel; and one, which had its stance by a little underwater glacis of sand, was light golden yellow. Did trout assume protective coloration in a few minutes, or were these colours derived from lying in habitual resting places? The spots along their backs were visible in the limpid flow: black with here and there one glowing vermilion in shafts of sunlight piercing the alder leaves high above the west bank. While I stood there I experienced a feeling that the day was fixed immortally, for ever, in blue space. For a moment I was back in the summer of boyhood. Water, mysterious water, was speaking to me again.

The cottage lay a little way outside the deer park, beyond a massiveness of lime trees and a tall iron gate. It was built of the usual Devon cob washed with lime, and stood on slightly sloping ground above, and away from, three smaller cottages which, we learned later, were occu-

Fishing Cottage

pied by workmen on the estate. A hasty look around inside, and we left to present ourselves to the agent, to de-
clare our eagerness to take both house and fishery for £30
annual rent respectively, and to pay all rates and taxes as
well. There were the usual formalities, of banker's and two
personal references to be provided; after which followed a
period of waiting, during which time we paid our second
visit to the valley.

What more could one desire, we said, as we gazed dis-
creetly over the garden hedge? Sunflowers and hollyhocks
grew against the lower casement windows. Behind them,
pear trees were held to the wall by staples. The buzzings
of wasps flying over our heads in two streams, past a summer house with conical thatched roof, made us wonder if
any pears would be hanging there on Michaelmas Day.
Apples with scabby faces hung green upon lanky trees in
the small orchard; perhaps we could make cider? The
summer air was still. High above the valley floated cirrus
clouds. Under the scattered white flakes a pair of buzzards
was soaring in wide circles, in draughts of warm air uprising from the earth. Their nest, perhaps, was in one of
the woods covering the hill behind the cottage.

Leaving my small son with his mother sitting beside the
deep pool in the deer park, I set out, with ash-plant, to
explore this new country. The way led up a timber-wagon
track among trees. Soon it was apparent that the plantations there were of different ages. One nearest to the
cottage, the roof of which now lay below me, had been
replanted in 1914, as recorded on an iron plate clouted to
an oaken post driven into the shaly ground beside the
track. The trees, therefore, had been growing for fifteen
years. Beyond these pale green Japanese larches and darker

spruces, as I approached the crest of the hill, was an older plot, almost black-green. The ride led into sunless glooms which darkened into silence; the spruces were over thirty years old, and coming to maturity, probably for telegraph poles. They had grown away so high in their regimentation that even the humming of the wind in their tops, together with the cries of crossbills and goldcrests, was shut out. Leaving the summer day behind me, I entered into a sombre world. All around were dark poles set with withered branches, rising out of a soil seeming dead and covered by pine needles, layer upon layer, dry and brown; but under the fallings of nearly a third of a century lay the seeds of rose-bay willow-herb and foxglove, those flowers of the graves of timber forests, which arise to conceal with their beauty the wreckage of arboreal life which has passed. There they were lying, awaiting their turn in darkness and silence; and imagining them there, ready to spring up into beauty with the light, when the timber should be thrown and hauled away, I felt the tunnels through the boles to be mysteriously glowing within their shades; and as I walked on, the breaking-out into sunlight again was almost too harsh, with its aspects of bracken and dried bushes of birch and furze stricken by billhook and slasher, to give growing space for a new plantation of larch and beech no higher than my little boy standing beside his mother on the ornamental bridge, far below.

No plaques for these post-war plantings; no money for them; the land had entered upon a period of depression. Prices were falling, and through difficult times the inheritance of many centuries must be preserved.

These fleeting thoughts passed, and in dazzling sunshine I examined a landscape of hills and woods, and the sun beginning to sink down upon the distant Atlantic. Immediately below me the meadows were studded with tiny black sheep and cattle. The tree-lined river was a wandering riband of lead, with white flecks revealing the rapid flow over shallows. I leaned upon my stick, content with the world.

To the north, where the valley narrowed and the park ended in iron railings arose a railway viaduct on stone pillars that were baseless, hidden by the foreground of growing beech and larch saplings.

The sun descending took my heart with it; I hurried down, and on the way home, I called at the agent's office, to be told that if conveniently I could come into town on the following market day, his Lordship would be agreeable to see me.

Thither in due course I went, to meet a shy old nobleman dressed in a well-worn dark suit. He had a mid-Victorian cavalry moustache, and in his faded blue eyes was an expression of one who had thought, and perhaps worried much, in a solitary and unvocal way. In a soft husky voice, and with the barest glance, he said that he had approved the application for my tenancy, and hoped that I would find everything to my wishes. I thanked him, and immediately took my leave with the agent to another room. There, almost totally enclosed within shelves of paper files and japanned tin boxes, I signed the lease, and then went outside to tell the good news to my wife and son. We were the tenants of the cottage, the fishing was ours!

After the equinoctial gales of Michaelmas, after the sad golden stillness of St. Martin's Little Summer—sad to the young man because the year was dying—the westerly winds brought much rain to the valley. During October I visited the cottage daily, with my manservant, to decorate and paint. It was nearly November when the family left the village by the sea and moved in with furniture, books and dog. By that time the last of the year's leaves had been torn away by roaring winds, the river was swilling along bank-high, plunging massively over the falls, turbid with washings from innumerable fields of arable and pasture as steep as they were small.

The valley was sombre at noon, and darkening into night by four o'clock under clouds bringing more rains from the Atlantic. My boots squelched through plashes of drowned grass in the deer park as daily I walked from the ornamental bridge to the falls higher up the river, to stand there while mist below arising from beaten waters hung damply on eye-lashes and the nap of my Connemara tweed coat. Well, I had wanted to escape from the noises of a village about which I had written all I knew in two books; and as the place was beginning to 'open up', as local councillors said—red iron-stone dust of the roads making the lime-washed cottage walls a faint pink from passing motor-cars—it had seemed good to depart.

Meanwhile, in one of the wettest autumns for half a century, daily I sought interest in new surroundings. Sometimes the way led over the hills, beyond the conifer plantations, or upon the moor, from which I returned wet and weary, gladly to change before a fire. Then, intent on a book, my walks were short, perhaps only as far as the railway viaduct, where usually arose a heron. One morning I saw my first salmon ascending the falls: a copper-coloured, lean fish which seemed to have little heart for the leap. It tried, with part-strength it seemed, again and again, after intervals for rest. Sometimes it rose along half its length out of the white mass of bubbles, only to be swept away. Once when its tail was clear as it rolled over, I noticed a rough red rosette in its flank, a wound about as big as a florin, and wondered if it had been shot. Surely shot from a cartridge, fired so close as to ball, would have shattered the fish? The puzzle remained unsolved until I heard of the existence of lampreys, or sucker fish, in the estuary.

Autumn was washed away into winter, and the melancholy of a dying year deepened. Would the rain never cease to drip from the thatch, would the plashes in the ruts of the estate timber-wagon hauled by Prince, Captain and Duke, lumbering with great trunks to the saw-mills, always gleam with water, and the garden remain undiggable and a tangle of weeds? Within the house it was cold when the frosts came, the winds driving under the doors of the sitting-room, in which a coal fire roared icily up the hole in the Victorian iron grate cast in the pattern of a shell. Behind the shell was, I believed, an open hearth. And in the deer park, under the oaks and beeches, were cords of fallen branches, lopped into lengths ready for loading into butts, as the short sturdy farm carts of that hilly country were called.

Making inquiries, I learned that some time in the past century three cottages had been made into one by the then clerk of works, for his own occupation. I imagined that in those days the iron grate was a coveted thing, to burn coal more conveniently than 'sticks' of oak and beech which smouldered under the iron crocks and kettles of labouring men's cots; but to me that octogenarian grate was inefficient, otherwise wasteful. Sitting before its flames, I wondered if it illustrated the principle of the refrigerator, the chilling function of which was, I had heard, induced by the heat of a flame causing a vacuum. The more coal that was shovelled into the cast-iron shell, the more the draught sucked past my body. In front, the roast; behind, the freeze. I spent the evenings in revolving slowly, as on a spit.

The watery world entered the leafless glooms of December. The frosts slipped into mud, as dim valley views were dissolved in more rain. From every walk by the river, again swirling over the stick-matted roots of drowned alders, one returned with sopping trousers and shoes. It was grand to feel the glow of blood within the body, to sip tea and play Delius's *Song Before Sunrise* on the gramophone; but afterwards, by the iron shell roaring up to join the distant thunder of the wind across the chimney pot, it was necessary, now and again, to jump about the room and flap the arms.

The clerk of works came round one morning, and after telling me much local history, including his grandfather's life in the house I now occupied, departed saying he would see what could be done. A week or two later a mason arrived and to him I gave my ideas of a hearth, saying that it must have a gradually sloping back to sharpen the upward draught, and throw forward the heat. There was a worn blue slate slab in front of the fireplace, and this would conduct the heat from the bricks of the hearth into the room, and make a pleasant place to stand in one's socks, after writing. For the feet grew cold while writing during the hours; and I remembered the shining steel hearth-plates in Pyrenean inns, on which beech and ash logs a metre in length burned, while peasants, having come in from star-sparkling frost outside, sat round the plate, their stocking'd feet upon its warmth.

I went away for a few days, and when I returned I saw that the slate was gone, and in its place a concrete slab, two days set. Concrete is not a conductor of heat; slate is; but after the initial disappointment, sharpened for the moment by a drive from London through frost in an open motor-car, thinking much of the time of my warm blue slab, the hearth became what a hearth should be. It burned wood slowly and threw out heat. I collected, and sawed up, many of the rough cords piled under or near the trees in the park. The cost to tenants of the estate was five shillings a ton. Beech made the best firing, then oak. Ruddy embers and yellow flames gave contentment to legs stretched out from a leather armchair, while the black iron kettle gently steamed as it hung from the serrated lapping crook on the chimney bar.

The blacksmith made me three trivets, with different lengths of pod or leg; and also a grill, upon which steaks, chops and kippers grizzled, before being picked out on a long iron fork, for supper in front of the fire. At times I repined that a mason's hammer had cracked up the slate slab, because, as he said, it was old. Possibly, I thought, two or three hundred years. It had been a lovely thing, deep blue and gentle, worn hollow in places with many feet resting on it, and mellowed with fat-speckles jumping out of how many cast-iron frying-pans of the past. Feeling for such old things was strong in me, also a sense of place; later I discovered a possible reason, in that my mother's family of Shapcote had lived only a few miles away, on the edge of the moor at Knowestone, at least ten generations before the heraldic visitations of 1610. A century after that date the place was sold, the family moved to Exeter, and Sarah Shapcote married an Irish post-captain in the navy at Plymouth called Thomas William Leaver, my great-great-grandfather. It was a good feeling that one had roots in Devon. Perhaps that was the basis of an instinctive feeling for the elements, and life created from those elements, of Exmoor.?

For four months the fire in the new hearth burned continuously. A slow draught, from a pair of Crediton-made bellows upon beech embers, and yellow teeth bit into logs taken from the wicker basket: the flames, around singing kettle, challenged the ice-patterns on casement window panes. Three good bucketfuls of potash, for the apple trees, lay within the hearth, for when daffodils and primroses would follow into light the lesser celandines, those floral morning stars. Already the sun below the plantation on the hill to the south in the deepest dark of winter was cutting a higher curve, and at evening Venus glowed above the deer park. The river, its jetsam piles of sticks bleached and dry, ran clear and green, fed by many springs gushing out of rushy hillsides, and down runnels upon rocky lanes and watercourses from the peat hags of the moor. It was a joy to stand on the ornamental bridge—now called by the family Humpy Bridge—and stare down at rushing water, while the kingfisher, bolting by in straight blue line, pierced the centre arch with its whistle.

The season for taking trout began on the first of March. I had neither rod, reel nor flies. Could I pierce, as with sapphire note of kingfisher, bird of flash and straight direction, the years of the war, that to me were not so much terrible, but years of such movement and excitation and comradeship that when they had passed the world had

Fishing Cottage

seemed poor and dispirited? The world was myself, I knew; but dare I try to return to a world still more remote, that of my boyhood before 1914, with its bright illusions and primitive joys? And there was a further reason for reluctance: I still had to re-create that life, through the imagination, with compassion and understanding. I carried the thought of it within me as a dark secret, hid from the light of day, my *doppel-ganger*.

The outward me felt happiness, after winter, that it was spring again; and I was young enough to think that the phrase of T. S. Eliot, *April is the cruellest month*, was without meaning. For when April of that year came, with its swallows; when the river was running glassy-clear, yet not so fast that the colours of the stones on its bed were indistinct; when over those stones, of all shapes and sizes, shadowy trout darted away as I walked upon the banks, suddenly I felt I must fish again.

The Boy Who Loved Fishing

When I went to live in the valley I was thirty-three years old. My knowledge of fish, and the life of a river, was slight. As a boy I had fished for roach and carp, in ponds and lakes, in country places in Kent and Bedfordshire that now were changed, with my exterior self, almost beyond recognition. Therefore I did not want to return to them; I wanted to cherish the feelings of romance and excitement when first setting forth with a cousin (who later was killed in the battle of the Somme) carrying bread paste and willow wand, with quill-float and line, to catch roach and rudd. We sat side by side on the bank of the pond hidden by reeds, until we moved to a more exciting place, the trunk of a fallen tree. I was seven years old; the place, a dozen miles from the county town of Bedford. Sitting on the tree trunk, a thrill of wonder ran through me the first time my quill, held down by two split shot, trembled, rose up, and went under. I struck so violently that the fish was jerked over my head into the cowslips of the meadow. The rosy fins of that roach, its white belly, the pale green scales, the golden eye! More joys were to come, for in the ivy of the tree above was a ring dove's nest, of black twigs thinly laid. I watched

22

one of my new friends, a carter's son, shin up and bring down two white eggs. I watched him blowing them, after piercing both ends of the shell with a thorn. I wanted them so much, but could not ask for them. After we had returned to the village, he offered them shyly at the gate leading past the stables to the courtyard, where a tall leaden pump stood, with a handle that went up far above my raised hands. The boy, who wore with pride a new celluloid collar, was a crow-starver during those Easter holidays, earning a shilling a week. How romantic it was to hear his wooden rattle, coming from the spinney of pine and beech in the brown, sloping field's centre, followed by faraway *Hullo-as*, as he drove away rooks from the spring-sown corn. He too died on the Somme.

Later days, in other woods and by rivers in Kent, with the great friend of my boyhood, fishing for carp and perch and gudgeon—the finest tackle for the small gudgeon, which loved a gravelly bottom—and once, in a river below the North Downs, clear-water worming for trout. Alas, the Darent was soon dead, killed by tar-acids which had run in after a thunder-storm; for it was the time when the white dust of roads was being laid by tar poured by hand from cans, to be brushed over by brooms which soon were clotted, and gravel was scattered from shovels. Soon, motor-cars no longer dragged behind them clouds of dust that made grey all the hedges. I did not know the Darent was dead; I thought I had hooked a trout. My line under the bridge was held fast by what I fancied tremblingly to be a big fish, which suddenly let go my brandling worm— so red between its yellow rings after scouring in damp moss since being forked out of 'a well-rotted dung-heap', as the book said. I think that perhaps I hadn't struck a fish after all, but a snag; but the feeling of excitement remained through the years.

It was a brandling which caught my first carp, in a lake where water-lilies lay in the low summer sun of early morning. Drops on their broad leaves glinted purple, red and green as a grey wagtail skipped upon the leaves, taking flies which had hatched. I accepted all this beauty as part of the wonder of life; but my ambitions were inspired by *Coarse Fishing*, by 'The Trent Otter', out of whose pages barbel, bream, tench and other fish inhabited my secret life. Of that sixpenny book in hard-board covers I knew the smells of the paper, the printer's ink, the binding; I knew every comma, some thicker than others, every yellow patch in the pages, as I sat with the Trent Otter during dark winter nights, under a fish-tail gas-jet in a room by myself, transported to the imagined world of deep-flowing Trent. Lying on my bed, I saw the barbel swims, I passed over them in an imaginary home-made canoe, on my way to the tent which awaited me with a camp-fire at its entrance. Therein I lay, on a bed of spruce branches, under the starry sky, while the moping owl in some ivy-mantled tower did to the moon complain, as the plowman plodded his weary way home. Gray's *Elegy* was my favourite poem.

When I was nine years old, I had my first bicycle, and in the years that followed I explored miles of unknown country during holidays from school. Reading and living were equal: my days were filled with romance in strange places where everything was seen for the first time. My life would go on like that for ever, in a world whose mysteries could never be solved.

·   ·   ·   ·   ·

The Boy Who Loved Fishing

Yet time must have passed through those long, long years, for how else had I become fourteen? Alas, I was fated to grow up. My secret life was guarded by over fifty blown birds' eggs, one of each kind, resting on sawdust in an old wooden custard box, with a hinged lid. Each speck and freckle and tint and shape of shell was known to me; each shell was the guardian of an adventure, part of the shining sky and woodland sun-dapple, returning upon me when I gazed at the talismanic shell. Beside the box lay my fishing tackle; a three-piece greenheart fly-rod stood in the corner of my room, beside the sections of a Thames roach pole, which when fitted together was twelve feet long. I could tap windows with it at night, without being suspected. I could point it at stars, and feel their light quivering down my arm. And one day, wonderful to be, I would fish in the Thames with it.

It was made of four lengths of bamboo, the butt or handle being massive, and the top rising to little more than the thickness of a match. The line, of finest plaited silk, was tied to a ring at the end. There was a quill float with its tip dipped in paint, and weighted with shot so that it was submerged all but the crimson end. Roach were shy feeders in the Thames (I had read) and so the hook must be small, a No. 12 or 14, knotted round the flattened end of the shank by a single white horsehair stained green, and held by a fisherman's knot to the silk line. On the hook a pellet of white bread flavoured with aniseed, or a scoured maggot; the long limp rod lifted, line and hook and quill wafted away from the bank, and let down twelve feet into the 'swim', where the quill float would fall sideways and sink away, all but that crimson tip.

The three-pound roach which one day I should hook

would not of course be hauled in, but the slender bamboo top joint allowed to yield with Chinese acquiescence until the fish was exhausted, and gently led in, its weight borne by the water, until the net lifted out this mighty monster of the Thames. Thus I fished in the pages of the Trent Otter, dreaming upon the counterpane in the light of the blue and yellow gas-jet.

I used my Thames roach pole twice. The first time was when I went after carp, whose back fins lay above the surface of the ponds fed from Caesar's Well during the long, hot, misty mornings of the summer holidays. Those ancient fish were nearly a yard long, their scales bigger than pennies, and almost as brown. With back fins loose and above water, they lay inert amidst squadrons of red-finned rudd, also motionless, but a few inches under the surface of the two-acre gravel pit. All day I sat upon the bank, upon exposed roots of pine trees growing to the edge, but never once did my crimson quill-tip disappear, leaving the line to cut a narrow angle on the water of exactly one-quarter of a right angle. I had read of that fact: the ship that ploughed the ocean also made an angle of twenty-two and a half degrees with its wake. My wind-light magpie-speckled silk line continued gently to billow; it never made an angle with the surface of the fish-ponds; the great foxes of the waters lay at doze, the rudd lay there too, unmoving throughout the still summer days of 1913. I was content; I was of summer everlasting, easily racing on the way home those monsters of the roads, the solid-tyred Tillings-Stevens motor buses, once feared by me as destroyers of the countryside I knew, but now part of the world of sun and joy.

In the early summer of the following year I was given

The Boy Who Loved Fishing

leave to fish in private lakes within a wood where peacocks called wildly and rhododendrons flowered under oaks. Above in tall hollies were dreys of red squirrels—always made of oak twigs, with their buff dry leaves, and sometimes an oak-apple. About these woods were pheasants of beautiful colours and strange shapes. I found the nest of a hobby, a little falcon with sharp wings of slate, which hurled itself forward in twisting speed as it skimmed the woodland rides, its creamy breast barred with dark brown below the proud all-seeing eyes. The nest was at the very top of an Indian spruce, too high for my climbing, though for a while I fancied myself as a falconer, taking a cast of eyasses and training them to get my food, as I lived wild in the woods, perhaps in a cave below one of the great oaks in the park, whose hollow trunk would conceal the smoke of my fire, ascending through a hidden pipe.

I had at my home two young kestrels, which I had tamed in a day. They flew down to me for food, and rode the least moving airs just over my head, hovering most delicately, plaintively, every flight feather adjusting itself to the breeze as anxious falcon-eyes stared down at me, their foster-parent.

In late July of that year I hid my Thames roach pole among the rhododendrons around one of the five lakes in that wood, until the next visit; for I was going to camp for the first time as a territorial soldier. I never saw the pole again, for one morning early in August general mobilization papers arrived, and I was away to other scenes, in which the old life seemed gone for ever. But it was not entirely so, as I was to discover in my first springtime in Devon after the war.

I Survey the River

One morning when, as was my habit about mid-day, I walked to Humpy Bridge, I saw several trout lying just under the top of the water. The sun was behind me, the stream ran glass-clear above the gravel. I could see their red spots as they wimpled the sur-face, taking something which was rising from the bed of the river. What could the insects be? A word heard in early years from my father who used to fish in his youth, came back to me. *Nymphs*. The fish, one behind the other, were taking nymphs as they swam up to hatch—or to die, within sight of their new element of air. I returned to get out the Morris Minor, keen to go into the town to buy rod and tackle. As I passed the road bridge I saw a motor-cycle in the ditch beyond, and looking over the parapet, saw a hatless figure in tweeds about to throw a fly in my water. He saw me at the same time, and hastening towards me, held out a hand in greeting, saying, 'Welcome to the district! The old tenant gave me permission to fish this part of the river whenever I wanted to, and I am sure you will extend to me the same privilege, won't you?'

I hesitated, then replied, 'Yes, by all means let me give you a day. I can't give more just yet, because I am not yet

28

I Survey the River

certain of my plans.' When I told him of my errand, he said, 'You could not have come to a better man!' and telling me the name of someone in the High Street, returned to the water with a wave of his free hand. I had no idea who or what he was, beyond the fact that he wore, with his rough tweeds, a collar by which I supposed him to be a curate.

The tackle dealer in the town combined this trade with the craft of a taxidermist. With him I had an informative talk about trout, artificial flies and wild life in the Devon countryside. He had, I gathered, a dislike of the idea of birds being shot and otters and foxes hunted, equal with a skill in mounting skin, pate and mask. In his shop he helped me choose a rod suitable for the higher waters of the river, a two-piece split cane, nine feet long and weighing four ounces, by Alcock of Reading. I thought it rather expensive at thirty shillings; the Thames roach pole had cost two shillings at Gamages; the cost of everything had gone up greatly since the war. But what was money? Quickly I bought a bronze reel, to balance the rod; enamelled silk line for the reel, a small aluminium box with a dozen flip-up mica windows, for flies, of which I picked a selection—Blue Upright, March Brown, Wickham's Fancy, Yellow Sally, and others whose names and colours took my fancy. A circular box of the same metal, with dual flannel lining, for keeping silkworm-gut casts pliable when fishing—of which I bought six, each nine feet long, as recommended by the dealer, who explained that the local rivers were usually fished with wet flies, which were 'swum' under-water, imitating nymphs, while dry flies imitated the hatched fly above the water. Finally I chose a collapsible net and wicker creel; and with a half-crown Conservancy

I Survey the River

Board licence to take brown trout from March 1 to October 1 in my pocket book, and the other purchases under the tonneau cover, drove back to the valley, imagining trout for dinner that night, with a bottle of hock from the little cellar under the stairs.

No time for luncheon when I got back. The midday rise was on! As coolly as possible I fitted up the tackle and hastened to the river. By the waterfall two hundred yards above Humpy Bridge, I dropped my team of flies into a swim, saw them sink, was gently pulling them against the current when a small trout rushed up from a submerged rock and hooked itself. Curving and flapping in the net, my fish had poppy-red spots among the black, a golden glisten of its flanks, and a hopeless eye. Leaving the rod against one of the beech trees, I ran home to show the catch to my son. The small boy, to whom the disastrous eye was pointed out, showed some distress; and to save the fish's life we went to the swamp at the bottom of the garden, and put it, already discolouring, in a small runnel of water. I declared that henceforward this fish would be his tame trout, his very own pet; but when I went back half an hour later, the fish was lying on its back, apparently covered with a thin film of wax. The wax was slimy. How ignorant of me to put it in dead water, void of oxygen! The fish had been asphyxiated; the mucus was its death-sweat.

I caught no more fish that afternoon, although I fished some way up the river above the viaduct. There I had a glimpse of the curate—as we called him among ourselves—fishing for the third time. By the time I got to where he had been, he had vanished.

. . . . .

I Survey the River

So I rediscovered the delights of water and of fishing. Once the clang of the lodge gate was behind me, and I was hastening under the limes where the bees sought murmurously for honey, my new life was one of anticipation, for what trout might I not see from Humpy Bridge? The view from the grey stone parapet was becoming so familiar that I began to regard the deer park as my own. And on a morning in May, how quiet and peaceful it was, standing on the bridge.

To the north, the wandering course of the river was marked by the alders on its banks, and in places by reflected sky. My stream was open for a score yards above the bridge to its first bend. There a diagonal tongue of gravel threw the current to one side. Over the bar the current hastened, musical upon innumerable shillets, as the flat pieces of rock were called. I had more than once waded across at that place, in water little more than a foot deep, but the pace of the stream was such that it rose bubbling to my knees. The ford was not yet come to low summer level.

Above the bend the river-bed was half the width at the ford, and correspondingly deeper. Trees grew on the steep right bank, where the rock was exposed. Yellow clay overlay the rock. The left bank was treeless and shelving; the main rush of water was upon the inside of the curve, so that the gravel brought down was not washed onwards, but thrown upon the outer curve. Flood after flood had left silt, gravel and sand there. The deposits made more narrow the low summer flow, so that it quickened under the alders. The quick flow kept the rocky bed bare. There trout lay when not feeding, in crevices and holes, while past them the stream moved with bubbles and swirls.

On the meadow side the banks of shillet prevented the

growth of seedling trees. I saw some start their two-leaved lives there, only to be ground away after floods, their tender stems stripped.

I spent much time kneeling, where the gravel bed shelved gradually, to see, through water clear as glass, how upon each flat stone was a colony of huts, or retreats, built of gravel specks cemented together. Within every shelter dwelled a crawling insect, whose head looked forth to eat the algae on its stone. The tiniest speck-houses held the larvae of the Dusky Midge, a minute flying insect which in hot, close weather of late spring drifted in clouds over the water. I had read that trout refused larger flies of dun and sedge when the midge was up; whereupon the angler, unless amidst his collection of feather, silk, fur and floss, was an imitation of the Knotted Gnat—imitating the love-flight or death-tangle of two of the midges—might as well save himself time, and stinging bites, and go home. Some-one had named it the Fisherman's Curse.

The mysterious curate, whom I met in The Fisherman's Arms, gave me further information. He said that although moorland trout were dashing, hungry little fellows, it was difficult to take them on the wet fly when the river was low. A freshet was needed: until then, the water was as good as dead. Why then, I asked myself, had I seen him on several occasions in the distance, apparently fishing my water? Perhaps he had divided the day I had given him into sections, twelve of two hours each, snatching at them as he travelled about his parish? I did not like to ask him this, lest he consider me mean. What an optimist! He must catch nothing at all.

Above the curving line of alders was a group of tall

I Survey the River

beech trees planted two, perhaps three generations before, in the age of landscape gardening, when the mansion of my landlord's family was built, within the deer park. The old, grey fortress-like home was on higher ground. Was it during this time that the river was straightened, and a series of artificial waterfalls made? Before, it had wandered from one side of the valley to the other. The bends were still marked by depressions in the pasture, at each bend a great oak.

Sitting under one of the trees, I imagined that at the former river-bend, amidst sticks, washed-out trees and other jetsam, acorns had been left. Cattle had eaten the seedlings; but one had grown beyond the reach of curling tongues that, like the wild red deer that came down from the moor to the valley in hard weather, pulled away its bite. Protected by brambles and vegetable wreckage, the seedling tap root went down, the stem rose with its first paired leaves, carrying up its shell. The bark grew tough, little branches went out; and after a dozen years, despite slasher and brushing hook, *Quercus Robur* was to stand, through the centuries, to grow bulging black and wide of arm, his roots spreading beyond the shadow of the mid-summer noon canopy; there to hold and slowly to decay; so that his hollows, above and below ground, gave shelter to otters, bees, mice and, by water-lapped toe-roots grasping earth, concealment for trout and salmon. Did the under-river roots perish? Was that why riverside oaks were often hollow?

A hundred and fifty years or more had passed since the straightening of the river. During that time a viaduct had been built, to carry trains to the town beside the estuary which eventually received the waters of the stream, mingled with scores of others flowing into the big river; the oaks which had marked the bends of the old bed grew the stronger with roots gone deep under packed beds of gravel, shillet, and the detritus of rocks worn in millions of years by water falling on its way down the valley.

At school one had been taught, a river swings from side to side in its valley. Looking at my river, I saw that, all the time, it was gnawing away, not only its bed, but its bank. Its current was pouring, pressing, scooping, using its gravel to abrade the valley bottom all day and all night. It was never still, never consistent in its pressures and shiftings. Its restlessness came from the shapes of its bed, from the differing waywardness of currents moving at every level. It was like a society made up of innumerable diversities of human beings at different levels, and therefore, perspectives. The river was always changing, ever striving to move objects resisting its flow. And every rise and fall of the water levels gave it new angles of attack upon the solids of the land. The spates piled up shillets and gravel, pebble by pebble, flake by flake, stone bead by stone bead, dropping each as it became heavier than the local water pressures, thus forming new barriers which narrowed the flow past old barriers. The gravel banks intensified the flow, which caused it to cut into the opposing bank, which was of soil on top and hard pan beneath—a pan that was one of the olden-time beds of the river, glomerate of stones, gravel, silt and clay, to be cut into anew, each particle to be gnawed until it dropped, to cause further obstruction, more dissension, more water-bickering. Water, like man, cannot be frustrated, by the nature of its energy; and like any human society, a river bed is always breaking down and remaking itself, and coming as it were to realize that

I Survey the River

the more its course changes, the more it discovers the past. River history is always repeating itself.

Leaving my place beside the river-relict oak, I walked over the meadow to look at the 'new' bed of the river, where it was straightened two or three generations before the period of my life beside it. Dams or weirs had then been built to modify the new flow, to give a series of gleaming terraces. At first much water must have been held back behind the mason'd barriers across the river. Long and deep pools were formed. Into them the freshets, or spates, shifted the shillets, with sand and silt during the fining-down periods. The silts dropped between the flat stones and bound them like mortar. As more shillets, sand and silt were brought down, every one an individual fragment of rock, moving gradually, jerk by jerk as it were, the pools became less deep, the new bed more consolidated, until thousands of tons of gravel lay behind each dam, making the water there shallower than it had been originally.

The stretch of water immediately above the fall where I had caught my trout was straight, shallow and plain. Walking upstream, I saw fingerlings darting away to the cover of rushy bank sides. Among them were a few larger fish, which seeing movement on the bank sank down to get the widest view; for the eye of a fish near the surface has the narrowest scope, since the top of the water is like a looking-glass, reflecting the bed of the river except directly above its eye, where the quicksilver is, as it were, rubbed away leaving clear glass.

Here the river flowed in an open, light-filled place. Across meadow-land arose the slopes of the valley. The meadows extended before me to the stone pillars of the railway viaduct, and as I watched, a train against the sky puffed slowly over, giving a little shriek as the engine entered a tunnel under the eastern hill. After this movement of civilization, I had the valley to myself once more.

The next waterfall had been built two hundred yards above the first. Most of it was washed away, exposing a foundation of mortar and stone, less than a foot in height, overgrown by water-moss. The moss was good holding for shrimp and nymph, I saw with satisfaction, having walked into the water. There was a gap in the middle of the foundations, through which water poured, not fast enough to cause whiteness, or bubbles, but with pace sufficient to fuse the looking-glass and so to dissemble the image of any stalking human figure. Seeing a fish rise before me, I ran back for my rod.

It was no good; my team of wet flies—Blue Upright at tail, Olive Dun dropper, March Brown bobbing near the loop of the gut cast—merely scattered them in that clear water. Once a salmon parr rose and snatched at the March Brown. It struggled more strongly than the trout, and I took it off the hook, holding it in my wetted hand lest heat scald it as it writhed and twisted. There was no triumph in hooking such a mite. Another parr jumped at a broken matchstick flipped into the water, after I had lit my pipe. I did not want to risk hurting them, knowing that if the barb pierced the white spiny tongue and drew blood, the baby was doomed. A parr was more gracile than a trout. Its tail-fin was forked. Among its red and black spots were vertical bars down its sides, like inky thumb marks. Without enthusiasm I went on fishing, casting clumsily, and giving up when one backward fling of my team of flies caught in brambles on the bank. Leaving my rod against an alder, I walked on, to note what banks were overgrown, particularly above the viaduct. As I was turning back, I saw the figure of the curate again, three hundred yards ahead. He vanished. I waited for him to re-appear, and when he didn't, I walked to where I had seen him. He was gone.

That afternoon, going into town, I asked the agent if I might cut some of the alders and hazel-nut bushes. He suggested that I arrange it with the tenant who rented the meadows above the viaduct. So on my return I went to see Farmer Aidgeboar, and said that, knowing how hard-worked he was, I was quite willing to cut down the trees for him. At once he found objections to this. Sharp stubs of hazel would prick the feet of his heifers. I said I would be careful to leave no sharp stubs. Also, I would like to buy the wood from him, as firing for my open hearth. Perhaps I could pay him for bringing it to the cottage? (I imagined a row of wooden wigwams seasoning for my open hearth in future winters.) He replied that he was stowed-up for time. Very well, would he consider hiring me his horse-and-butt to carry the firing home? My man and I could do the work together.

'But supposin' th'ould 'oss drops dade?'

'I'll get you another.'

'Gordarn, supposin' your man or you was to cut your-self with the axe, where'd I be then over this yurr Wuk-man's Compensation muddle?'

'All right, then. Will you have the trees felled, and deliver the wood to me, and charge what you think right?'

'Gordarn, I ban't got no axe, midear!'

'I've got one.'

'Mebbe you have, but this be no job for a kid's chopper!'

'My axe has a seven-pound head.'

'Aye.' He stared at me. Then energy created in opposition to the elements made him say, 'But what about th'ould 'oss? Tes a bit lame-like, and these yurr cruelty people are particular nowadays!'

Farmer Aidgeboar and I left it at that for the time being. He *zuck-zuck'd* his pony, and trotted away southwards, his long legs hanging to his boots near the ground; while I returned to the valley, to continue my exploration northward. According to the map of oiled paper, marked in red ink, which was attached to my tenancy agreement, my bit or beat ended a quarter of a mile above a boundary bridge.

The river now entered a tunnel of trees meeting overhead. Parting the branches, I saw that the water moved wildly, gushing here, gliding there on its bed of rock. After three hundred yards the tunnel opened, there was a deep pool at the bend, shaded by the canopy of a sentinel oak.

At the throat of the pool I saw five small black and white birds squatting on a rock. They jerked their tails as they prepared to fly, or dive, from sight of my face and hands parting hazel branches. Quietly withdrawing, I saw them speeding away as I walked on, to where the river opened wide at the next bend. Under its spreading oak this pool was more shelving; and to my excitement I saw what surely must be a salmon shooting away, over pale gravel which gave a clear view of limpid water. The bow-wave spread towards the throat of the pool, where the tumbling waters jostled white. I heard the sound of its acceleration as it sinuated itself forward, springing away as it were from its own bended bow, from first one side, then the other. Then the bow-waves were lapping under the roots of the oak.

I Survey the River

Recently I had bought some old copies of *The Salmon and Trout Magazine*, wherein I had read that the fins of a fish were for balance, or trimming; while the paired-fins forward of its belly were for holding, like hands. The caudal or tail-fin was for steering, and also for helping the sinuation of forward movement. I stood there watching to see if the big fish would return, for the throat of the pool was shallow. Would it shoot down-stream, passing me where I stood in the water? But no long leaden shape drove down. The salmon lay hidden under white tumbling water; and not wishing to make known its presence there (for a cottage or lodge stood fifty yards away) I sat down upon the bank, to lift my feet and empty my shoes of water and gravel.

Exhilarated by the feel and sound of water, I continued my exploration, coming to where the stream hurried, with foamy jags and tassels of water over and past brown rocks. Ferns grew there, and plants of water celery; but the sight of coal ashes, egg-shells and potato peelings, together with empty tins and bottles lying down the river bank and in the river, obviously a domestic rubbish tip, was not pleasing.

Trying not to think of this limpid river as an ash-tip, I walked on, coming to swampy meadows where clumps of rushes grew amidst rust-scummed water-plashes. It was deadly water for fish, but the delight of snipe, which arose with sceaping cries as they darted away in erratic flight. Then immediately before me a heron, grey and big, yellow-beaked, flapped up like a feathered windmill, dropping the contents of its gut with exertion and fear. I knew him to be the enemy of small fish, eating more than his weight of trout and parr every day; despite that, he re-

I Survey the River

mained but skin and bone, loosely centred upon those vast quills and hollow bones, some of which, making his shoulders, were extra air-space for his lungs. I told myself that I must not feel too ungenerously towards this Old Nog, for had he not earned me $500 for a short story about him in 1924, published in the United States, just before I was married? And so helped me to finish a book about an otter, which had brought me to where I was at that moment, the tenant of this paradisal water? The balance of nature was akin to the balance of a man's feelings. Over the trees flew Old Nog, neck tucked in, feet held straight behind him, wings flapping like borrowed sails from an ancient windmill, his voice an ungreased spindle—
Kaa-aa-r-k!

Herons, I knew, fished for eels. Eels ate trout spawn, those tiny grape-like eggs, by no means caviare to the general predators of the stream. Eels, too, ate fry and fingerlings. Eels attacked low-water-locked salmon, tugging at their gill-rakers, eating them alive. *Toujours la balance*—the heron glided down to the river half a mile below me; it pitched, and looked around for some minutes, and then tottered to the water.

Now the river slowed and deepened into what looked to be a wonderful pool below a bend. The rocks so lay that the force of the river had removed the gravel about them, depositing broad beds of it upon a stretch below, amidst which were islets of grass and willow. Among them the water broke into several shallow streams, each bubbling and murmuring. Here grew green water-plants of hollow-stalked *umbelliferae*, holding to the sand between the stones and the silt. Wading in, I saw that the roots of these plants

40

I Survey the River

gave shelter to shrimps and caddis worms. At my appearance a shoal of trout sped away from the shallows into
deeper water ahead. Then a bright cry as of silver wire
enamelled sapphire filled the watery shade. It came from a
kingfisher, alarmed by my presence in the water. Straight
and fast it was gone, a sight that opened the heart, and
made the spirit free as the sky.

Still walking northwards, I saw before me a bridge bearing a narrow lane over the river. A stone in the centre of
the parapet marked the boundary between two parishes.
Above, my fishing was from the right bank only, according to the map on my agreement.

With satisfaction I noted that this right bank was fairly
free of bushes, while an open meadow extended away from
the water. Also that my side of the stream had a stony
verge below the bank, which would give good standing
room, also cover for my body when fishing there.

The left bank, on the contrary, looked most unattrac-
tive. It was covered with brambles, and thickets of alders,
which would make the casting of a fly difficult, if not impossible. My one-bank-only, therefore, was practically
both banks.

I was musing thus happily when I saw two figures
coming towards me on what I considered to be my side
of the river. The first carried a rod. Behind him was a
youth with a net, and wicker creel slung over his shoulder.
Ah, poachers! I thought, seeing dock leaves sticking out of
the hole in the lid, through which fish were slipped; and
around the hole were scales and traces of blood. The creel
looked to be heavy, too. I must be wary, watch my step,
keep my equal-mindedness. I greeted him affably, opening
what I fancied to be a forthcoming verbal duel by a

remark that the river, no doubt, was rather low for fishing.

'Rather low for fishing? Bob, open up the basket!'

Within were layers of fish the size of small herrings. Their spots were dulled; dark stains on the backs of their heads extended past their gill-covers. The youth laid them out on the meadow. I counted eighteen, and inquired if all had been taken above the bridge.

'Yes, indeed, and I'd have three times as many, if the water had not been over-fished. What you see there is what I would have taken out in an hour, a few years ago. Now it's a morning's fishing. Some so-called sportsmen nowadays seem to be out only for the size of their baskets.'

He went on to say that, if I looked in the fish book at The Fisherman's Arms, I would see an entry made by one visitor that he had already taken out of Devon streams one thousand, two hundred and forty-nine fish that season.

'He's a theological student, rusticated by all appearances, who is fishing mad. If you come across him, look out! Last season he cribbed from me my method, which kills fish when nobody else considers it worth while to fish. The generally accepted idea is that it's no good fishing when the water is as low as it is now.'

He unpicked the barb of a small red-whisker'd object from the cork of his rod handle, and let it float in the breeze. I could see that it was tied to the most slender gut. He lifted the rod point so that the fly strayed near, and catching it, showed it to me.

'Look at the shining hackles! Look how it rides! It's deadly in low bright water. Do you see how the gilt round the shank of the hook is ragged? That's from the teeth of the trout which have snapped at it, sucking it in, so eager are they to get at it. In fact, many of the rises are short, slashing rises, so that they strike with the tail. The colour of the hackle makes them angry, I fancy, and they dash at it in rage. At least, that's my theory, because quite a number are foul-hooked, sometimes in the tail. Would you care to let me show you how to fish with it? I call this fly The Poacher.'

I asked him whether he meant below the bridge, or where he had been fishing already. He replied, indicating the river behind him, that the water above Boundary Bridge was no good; it was fished-out. The Fisherman's Arms, he said, had four rods on it; two kept for guests staying there, or day-tickets, and two which he had for himself.

'I suppose all four rods have been fishing from my bank, because it is open?'

'Your bank?' He pointed to the uncut and unlaid jungle across the river, and said, 'That's your bank, my dear sir!'

'But that is the left bank, surely? Mine is the right bank, according to my agreement.'

'You forget that the banks of a river are defined by looking towards its mouth, not towards its source! I have two rods for the rest of the season, but I'm going away after midsummer. You can have my tickets then, if you like, and fish from the meadow.'

I thanked him, and said that I hoped he would fish my water when it was convenient to him. Perhaps he would let me watch him using his dry-fly method.

'I'll be going away for a fortnight, to fish in Cornwall, but I'll come over and try your water, if you like, on my return.'

Two days later, while standing on Humpy Bridge, I saw

the iron gates of the park being opened by the lodge tenant, and my landlord riding through. We had already been honoured by a call at the cottage, and an invitation to luncheon at the Big House, as the other tenants of the hamlet called it. They also spoke of him as the Lord of All, while the heir was the Young Lord.

The Lord of All was a shy man; and his shyness affected what, at that time, I thought of as my chameleonic nature. I wondered if I should remain upon the steeply arched bridge, lest his mount, an animal of blood, be startled by my unaccustomed figure there, and rear up, perhaps throwing its rider? Hoping that my action would not be interpreted as reluctance to meet my landlord, I left the bridge and went down to the bank, ostensibly to look at the nesting hole of a lesser spotted woodpecker chipped out of the bole of an alder. This bird puzzled me. I had heard it making a rapid drumming noise in the early spring, sounding as though the bird were striking, as rapidly as machine-gun fire, a dead branch of an oak. The throbbing noise resounded in the deer park. How could so small a bird produce such a series of vibrations? Did the dead oak bough amplify the drumming noise of its tongue, or was its beak striking the actual wood? The bird, black and white and red, was hardly so big as a sparrow, yet from it came sounds audible half a mile away.

While I stood beside the nesting hole there came, magnified by echo through the bridge, the noises of a horse's feet on submerged gravel, and looking down through the reflections of ripples playing on the arch, I saw the old nobleman crossing by the ford which gave its name to the hamlet.

Returning to the bridge, I was in time to see him lay

I Survey the River

the reins on his horse's neck and walk his mount towards me. In a dry, slightly throaty voice, and giving me no more than an occasional glance, he said, 'Good morning. I understand you saw the agent about restocking the river. He tells me that it has been over-fished. Have you taken many trout this season?'

I replied that I had taken one; but the river was low for the wet fly.

'Yes, rain is needed. I have proposed to pay one-third of the cost of re-stocking, the total cost not to exceed thirty pounds. Is that agreeable to you?'

I thanked him, and having inquired about my wife and children, he bade me good morning and rode away, a spare, almost austere figure wearing dark jacket and trousers of the same material, his legs below the knee en-wrapped in black leggings with straps. His horse moved with the South African triple-canter, a graceful, easy motion across the grazings of the park, in the midst of which was enclosed the village cricket pitch, where on Saturday afternoons matches were played, seen by me from a distance.

I hastened home to tell the good news. That afternoon we went to visit a trout farm over the border, whose advertisements I had seen in *The Fishing Gazette*, which I received once a week with my newspaper.

I Visit a Fish Farm, and Meet Poachers

Wearing goggles and flying helmets, windscreen flat, pale green beechen hedges beside the road rushing past, we drove eastwards to the valley of the Barle, of which Richard Jefferies, spiritually the most piercing of writers upon English country, had described in one of his books fifty years before, in a rare mood of relaxation in a life of continual struggle and poverty.

The brown Barle river . . . enjoys his life, and splashes in the sunshine like boys bathing—like them he is sunburnt and brown. He throws the wanton spray over the ferns that bow and bend as the cool breeze his current brings sways them in the shade. He laughs and talks, and sings louder than the wind in his woods.

Anthropomorphic nonsense, wrote one barren critic fifty years after Jefferies's death, declaring that a river was not a man. But a river is part of a man, even as music is also part of a man, and a river lives as a man lives; and both can die. A polluted stream, the bright spirit of water dead, is as sad as human death from murder. The soul of the murderer has been murdered first, we know; let the

I Visit a Fish Farm, and Meet Poachers

rivers sing, let the algae be sun-brown, let us pray that the black slime of death, with the bubbles of chemical strangulation, will never come upon the Barle as, temporarily, upon rivers elsewhere in England.

'Looney Dick', as Jefferies's neighbours called the young man, heard the laughing of the Barle running down from the moor, in the 'eighties of last century, when visitors walkéd on foot from the railways stations, or rode by carts, coach and saddle. If ever the dead befriended the living, Jefferies was my friend in youth; and this day, as we rushed into the scent of furze upon the high ground, I thought gratefully of him.

Along the road over the ridge our new sports-car fled, moulding itself to the road rising and falling between tall beechen hedges. The umbral hues of the moor were slightly lessened by sunlight to the north: whortleberry leaves were springing there, the hues of wine coming upon their leaves, amidst rising ling and bell-heather. When we stopped, the bubbling sweetness of curlews floated in the air.

Sometimes in the past, when approaching one of the several little country stations on the Somerset line from Taunton, many of them grown with roses and other flowers, I had glimpsed an area of rectangular fish-ponds as the train began to slow. Once I had seen fish leaping out of rectangular waters ringed and rippled by rises. There, hundreds of thousands of trout—Rainbow, Loch Leven and Brown—were hatched and reared every year.

It was too late in the season to see the eggs, on that May afternoon. The eggs had arrived there in the past autumn, having been stripped from wild fish netted in a lake near Taunton. The ripe hens had been held over a bucket and

47

squeezed by expert hands until most of the eggs were dropped; and after release, all passion spent, the fish had been allowed to swim away in the lake. Had they, later, gone through the motions of spawning, cock fish by hen's side, but vacantly?

For the cock fish, before being put back, had been held over other buckets, and their milt worked out. Afterwards the milt had been poured on the eggs and stirred gently; then they were brought to the hatchery.

There the eggs were laid either on glass rods in series, or on perforated zinc trays within shallow troughs. These were covered from the light, while water from the river, which had passed through filter-beds of coke and gravel, trickled slowly over them.

After a few weeks dark specks appeared within the eggs, which were about the size of sweet-pea seeds, but opalescent. Known as eyed-ova, it was safe to send them, packed in wet moss in box or tin, as far as South Africa and the United States.

Most of the eyed ova remained at the hatchery, in zinc trays within troughs of tarred wood. Week after week, by day and by night, water flowed gently from one trough to the next, each trough slightly lower on the tables than the one above it, during winter and early spring. The eggs were inspected regularly, for fungus disease and infertility —those eggs which had become opaque and yellow must be removed at once.

One morning it was seen that an egg-case, like a diminutive grape skin, was floating loose by the perforated zinc barrier of a tray; and an alevin, about half an inch long, was trying to conceal itself under the eggs. Thereafter hatching became general. Two or three alevins in every hundred were deformed, with curved spines. These poor creatures were easily seen, as they spun round and round instead of wriggling forward into the mass crowding for concealment to the corners of the tray.

It took about three weeks for the sac under an alevin, the equivalent of a yolk, to shrink and become its belly. The little fish, called a fry, would then begin to poise itself in the water, head to stream, and watch for anything that passed. Now was come the time for transference to larger troughs, where they were fed on finger-pinches of powdered liver.

Later they went outside to the fry pits, there to await the regular showers of larger food. Visitors to the fishery were usually warned against going near the pits, as the wavery, foreshortened and distorted image (the underwater view) of a human being excited them, and they dashed at one another. Indeed, it was not unusual for a more developed fishling to seize its neighbour and retire to the bottom to gorge it, head first.

The fry, now between an inch and an inch and a half in length, grew unevenly. Bigger fingerlings were separated. At one year they might be from three to six inches long. The two-year-olds and three-year-olds we saw cruised violently when they spied us on the grassy banks; the fishmaster scattered a spoonful of food: the surface boiled and broke: black-spotted backs appeared with tails and greenish flanks: pallid mouths opened.

Pointing to the black zinc grill, the fishmaster said, 'Do you see those minnows, where the water enters? They've managed to get in from the leat, which brings the river water into our field, through the filter beds. Why they aren't taken is a mystery.'

I Visit a Fish Farm, and Meet Poachers

I wondered if the trout were used to food appearing in the pool centre only, and knew no other feeding habit. Then I asked the fishmaster what fish he advised turning into my water.

'We usually suggest fingerlings, or two-year-olds.'

When we had arranged a dispatch, he told me that one of the pits held salmon parr, hatched from eyed ova sent down from the Tay in Scotland. They looked like small trout, with black and red spots. Adult Tay fish, he explained, were hog-backed fish, with small mouths, unlike the Exe salmon, which were long and lean. If the instinct to find its way back to the parent river was in the egg, he said, the parr now in the pit, after their release as two-year-old smolts would find their way back to the Tay. If, on the other hand, fish had an individual memory, or sense of place, some would return to the Barle.

'It will be an interesting experiment,' he said. 'We shall know the Tay fish, because they are thick-set, with hog-backs. The Barle fish are long, and comparatively thin.'

The idea was exciting. First the alevin; then the fry; the parr at two years and some months after hatching becoming a smolt in a silver coat—and returning not to Tay, North Britain, but Taw in Devon, a salmon faithful to its nursery water! I asked if I might buy next season some Tay eyed ova, and the fishmaster promised to send me some.

He told us of his worst fear for his fish: pollution. How his predecessor had been broken by it, when one August, during a thunderstorm, the sewage tanks of a town beside the river up the valley had been emptied; but the 'fresh' was local, and limited, surface water only; and all the sludge, borne upon one wall of water, came down the leat by which water entered the pits from the river. At once the filter-beds were choked. Pouring into the pits, the effluent asphyxiated every fish within a few minutes. The owner sued the town council, and won his claim for damages. The town council appealed, and the decision of the Petty Sessions Judge was reversed. Thereupon the owner appealed. The High Court allowed his appeal. The town council once more appealed. The Appeal Court reversed the High Court decision. The owner carried his case to the Lords. The Lords reversed the Appeal Court decision, and awarded the owner a few hundred pounds damages. By this time he was broken in health. He sold his ruined business and died soon afterwards.

'Now your friend the otter is a jovial beast compared with some of our fellow-men,' went on the fishmaster. 'Once an otter got into the pits here, and played merry hell. The otter hounds got *him* all right!

'Then there are kingfishers, but we don't object to them. They're pretty birds, and add to the gaiety of nations. Another worry in summer is heat. Warm water rapidly loses its oxygen. Algae grow in heat, too, and absorb oxygen. We put up shades of hessian on wooden frames, but we have to watch for signs of disease. We need a spate now, one is overdue. Soon the small maiden salmon, from four to seven pounds, will be coming in from the sea, but they won't be able to run up from the estuary in this low water.'

He pointed to the Barle running noisily over the stony stickles below the bank at the end of his fishery. It was time to depart. Seeing us to our motor, he confirmed the order.

'We will deliver in galvanized tanks, with ice in them, as oxygen reserves, by lorry. We'll dispatch your fish tomorrow: three hundred yearlings at a shilling, that's £15. One hundred two-year-olds at half-a-crown, that's £12 10s.

I Visit a Fish Farm, and Meet Poachers

Three large fish, two Loch Leven, one Brownie, at half a guinea each, say £1 10s. Total, £29. Right. We'll reach your place about half-past ten. Yes, your three big fish will be all right in that deep pool below the ornamental bridge. The water there can't support such big trout, but if you feed them, they will remain, otters and poachers with night-lines permitting, and spawn in your gravel beds in autumn, and then return to the pool. They'll be your stock fish. Before you go, have a look at our tame fish in the leat.'

Past the fishmaster's cottage ran a rapid gravelly stream. It was about a yard wide, and seven to ten inches deep. In it long bines of water-crowsfoot waved and rippled, bright green and glass-clear in the corrugated water. He threw in some food like small broken dog's biscuit, and waves travelled up the swift flow preceding big fish, back fins out of water, mouths open. I wondered if I could dig a leat and fix some grills in it, taking water from the runner at the bottom of the swamp below the garden, and keep fish there, perhaps in a pit. And of course fish in the Bridge Pool as well. With such ideas, I said goodbye; and with windscreen flat, climbed up to the crest of the ridge and rushed westward again, between the tall beechen hedges yellow-green with their masses of new leaves, down the road that led eventually to the Atlantic coast, and the salmon that came in from the sea.

When the lorry arrived my small son and I, with his mother, went out and watched as the tanks were lifted down, ice still floating above many fish curving in layers as the water swashed and slopped. First the three large trout, quite fifteen inches long, were taken to the bank

I Visit a Fish Farm, and Meet Poachers

below the pool, where cattle had grooved a way in the clay to drink. There, river water was poured from a can into the tank, to bring the temperature of the river gradually to the cold ice-water, to prevent shock. Then the moment when the tank was tilted, water pouring out; and, as it went on its side, river water poured in, the fish slithered out, sinuating away over stones into deep water —their new home.

I peered down from the craggy parapet above, to see no fish shadows below; but a handful of dry food, from the little parcel in the lorry, soon had one yellowish and two greenish flanks rolling up. It was then I realized my mistake: for we were going to put fifty two-year-old Loch Leven fish in that pool. When they joined in the dash for food, would not the flashes lure the three-pounders to seize them?

A suggestion was made to put the fifty smaller fish above the bridge. Therein was good holding, for the west bank was bound by the roots of alders, which flourished in the water, grew entwined, and floated, making caves for hiding. So into the shelving water the next tankful went, after what the lorryman called equalizing the water temperature, and at once the gliding surface was broken by the skipping out of blue-green fish, intensely black-spotted, with small yellow and chocolate squares among the black.

Later, these fish were to develop vermilion spots among the black, including the crimson dash on the little rear fin upon the back forward of the tail. The books called it the adipose fin, to me it was a pennant.

The lorry moved slowly on the farm road to the first waterfall, where grew the tall beech trees. In the pool below fifty more two-year-olds were soon skittering about in the shadowed water. They were shocked and exhilarated by the oxygen from the bubbles bursting under the weir, and perhaps by the taste of peat: for my stream rose upon the moor, not far from the singing Barle.

A further tankful of yearlings, finger size, went in three parties into the shallows above the fall: the first lot, immediately above, the second a quarter of a mile onwards, the third in the big pool below the railway viaduct, where jackdaws cried and tumbled above in the blue. Down on earth there was the smell of honey, for bees also had their nests under the steel and wooden railroad supported by the lofty stone pillars.

At evening I wandered up the river. Below the viaduct my stream made a turn, the last of its own making before the old-time straightening and terracing. It was, I thought, the best pool on my beat. Immediately beneath it was another pool, one-third of it in eddy, where the water turned back like a wheel under the far bank. Here much gravel was deposited by floods; beyond were piles of sticks on a rocky ledge, the entire place being shadowed by great oaks. I stayed there, in the warm darkness, beside the pool. There came the play of fire on the steam of engines rolling over the viaduct: a ruddy glow was reflected upon the water. Henceforward I thought of the pool as the Fireplay, and the lower pool as the Wheel.

I sat there while an evejar reeled among the bracken, and flew after moths, planing across my vision with wings held high, and at a tilted angle; while the rings of fish rising in the Fireplay, where my new Loch Levens had settled down, and were taking sedge-flies, were drawn away by the water. I sat there while the stars wheeled westward over the viaduct, and a mist moved down the valley; then it was time to go back to the cottage, and light the oil-lamp in my reading room, and think, as I lay back in my leather armchair, of the river now filled with fish.

During the following week, while wandering down St. James's Street in London, I bought what I thought was the proper equipment for a fly-fisherman—mackintosh waders to the thigh; worsted stockings to cover the feet and prevent abrasions by gravel when the canvas brogues, set with nails, were strapped on; waterproof jacket with many pockets, cut in the Norfolk style; Harris tweed hat with brim to keep off rain, and band around which to enwind spare gut casts, amadou (dried tree-fungus) with which to dry soaked hackle flies; grease box with which to make them buoyant; knife with many gadgets—corkscrew, scissors, spike for piercing the heads of fish too big for their necks to be broken (only a bad fisherman left them to die slowly of asphyxiation, I had read), file to sharpen the barbs of hooks, and the usual blades. Also a bottle of highly volatile oil in leather case, with boxwood top to the cork (in which was set a little brush, with which to dab under my ears and on my temples) to keep away midges. This was hung from a jacket button. Now, I thought, I was ready to start my initiation into the art and mystery of a dry-fly purist.

The morning of my lesson came at last. My tutor arrived, with the youth called Bob, by taxicab. He carried with him to our threshold a log basket, which he presented to me, saying he hoped it would serve me as well as it had served him. He was soon leaving for the Antipodes, where he was making his home, among the gigantic trout of New Zealand. Fishing in England, he said, was finished.

Soon afterwards I began to wonder if fishing in my stream was finished. For to my wife he offered some fish wrapped in a cloth, as he did so he said to me, 'I took these this morning in The Fisherman's Arms water, north of your beat, where first we met. You'll be surprised,' he went on, unwrapping them, 'that your taking over the water here appears to have coincided with a new run of estuarial trout! Several other fishermen report that they have taken fish like them.' He opened the cloth to reveal about a score of my two-year-old Loch Levens. Prodding one he said, 'Obviously estuarial feeding produced these yellow spots. In Ireland they would be called slobs. Small for slobs, I admit, but plainly they have been feeding in salt water. Yet the curious thing is that their flesh isn't pink. The flesh of brown trout feeding in salt water, owing to shrimps and prawns and gravel sprats, turns pink. They're the peal, you know. These little fellows have flesh of a tallow colour. There's a distinct flavour to them, if a trifle muddy. I've sent a scale up to Fishmongers' Hall, to have it read. Try frying them in smoked-bacon fat. Olive oil spoils the delicate flavour.'

My small son had gone pink in the face. He frowned. Then looking at our guest he said accusingly, 'Those are my father's fish!'

'Or were,' I hastened to explain, 'until they travelled up-river a couple of miles.'

'News of them has travelled, too. Several rods from the pub, as I remarked, have brought baskets back. In fact, word has got round, and Harn at The Fisherman's Arms has had many applications for day tickets.'

I Visit a Fish Farm, and Meet Poachers

Having eaten some of the ex-hatchery fish for luncheon —their eyeballs turned white and sepulchral in the frying-pan—I asked our guest if he knew of any larger trout having been taken, adding that I had put in some three-pounders.

'Good God, if you'll pardon the expression! *Three pounders!* They'll turn cannibal! They'll clear out every fish in the river!'

I thought that at the present rate of removal, they would starve before they had a chance of becoming cannibals.

'Wait till the rain comes, then take my advice, and get them out with a spinner, in cloudy water!'

'My lease permits fishing by fly only.'

'Who's to know? You pay for the fish, don't you?'

Beside the river he put up rod and reel, greased his enamelled line for floating, tied on a gut cast, and then a fly. This he greased, afterwards fluffing out its rufous hackles.

'There's The Poacher! Jolly little fellow! Red game-cock hackles, tied with gilt wire. Three whisks. Don't put on too much grease—it's paraffin wax, you know—just enough to waterproof the hackles and make the fly ride high. Brush the hackles lightly between thumb and finger, like this. They should stand out like a floating thistle-seed, all round the clock. The fly should ride down the water well cocked-up, irresistible. Just watch. Stand beside me. Go away, you boys, keep out of the backward sweep of the fly! Or you'll be hooked.'

My elder son rapidly removed himself once again with a frown. The younger boy, not yet two, stood still, mild wonder in his eyes, as unemotional as he had been at birth.

My tutor pulled out line, the while he waved the rod,

keeping his elbow well into his side, so that the spring of the rod against his thumb did the work. 'Just imagine you've got a whisky bottle under your arm. Now watch me.'

The fly was now sailing to and fro above our heads, not violently, not as a whip would be cracked, for that might flip it off by cracking the bended gut, which soon became dry and brittle in the air, he explained. Then, with a final forward throw, which took with it a spare loop of line pulled through the bronze snake-rings, the fly sailed forward and floated down, and touching the glassy water, was leapt at by a salmon parr and drawn under. With a flick the barb was driven into the corner of the bony mouth, the struggling fish lifted out, and grasped in a broad hand.

'Do you think it a good thing to wet one's hand before touching undersized fish?'

'Waste of time, in my opinion. Far too many parr in the river. Take food of trout. They're a nuisance. The more out the better.'

The lesson lasted about an hour, while the instructor caught several trout, as far as the viaduct. There he announced that the sun was too bright, fishing would be better in the evening, when the spinners came on the water. Anyway, he remarked, no fisherman liked being watched. He must go. He was kind enough to give me two of his special flies, and say where I could get them copied, at the shop in the High Street I had already discovered.

'Now you try my method down here. Practise it. Don't go up-river, you'll get entangled. You're an apprentice. I've taken advantage of your offer to fish your water, by

I Visit a Fish Farm, and Meet Poachers

the way, and am staying for a couple of days in the cottage near Boundary Bridge. Good day to you.'

For the next two days we ate hatchery trout for breakfast, lunch and dinner; fried in olive oil; bacon fat; beef dripping; plain, kippered and dipped in oatmeal after splitting. Blanched eyeballs reproached me three times a day.

Meanwhile I had returned to the hatchery to buy a hundred-weight bag of fish-food—like small-broken dog biscuits mixed with shredded dried horse-flesh. The fish in the pools leapt to it. The fishmaster told me that daily feeding would hold them there. I future, I determined, no one should fish for my tame trout.

On the evening of the fourth day after my lesson, thinking that my tutor had gone. I decided to try my new dry flies in the pool below Boundary Bridge. In uniform and with accoutrements, I trudged thither, to find him standing in the river below the pool. I sat down and watched him; but after a few minutes he called out, 'A fly fisherman is like a heron, uneasy when watched!'

I withdrew to the viaduct, where columns of ants were arriving to gorge on a patch of honey on the cart track beneath. More drips were coming down, the honey-flow was strong that year. High above the structure seven buzzards were soaring in circles, stepped up like the sails of a full-rigged ship. The evejar began its first reeling noise in the bracken of the slopes leading to the hilltop plantation of spruce and larch, the young moon hung in the sky.

The following evening I went by motor to Boundary Bridge, to try the stickles below the salmon pool. There alders screened the shallows noisy with a thousand tongues of water, willow grew on little islets amidst the gravel, with tall water plants. I was about to take my rod out of its case when I saw him, working upstream, cat-like, moving slowly from run to eddy, from eddy to stickle. So I withdrew, and sat some distance away, to rise and go towards him as he climbed the bank.

'You're a funny chap, 'pon my soul,' he said. 'Don't you usually go to greet your guests when you see them?'

Apparently he was not feeling heron-like that evening. I never saw him again. His tuition enabled me to enjoy many a happy hour with the dry fly, including two of a variant pattern I discovered in an old book, by a doctor who wrote on the art of fishing in rapid streams. He, too, had used the buzz type of floating fly. As for the curate, I never saw him again, either.

That summer, having taken several dozen good fish with the single hackle fly, I decided that what was needed was a smaller, lighter rod, with which to fish under the trees above the viaduct (which remained uncut, as Farmer Aidgeboar could not make up his mind). Such a rod was made for me in London by Westley Richards. It was of split-cane, weighed two ounces, and was seven feet long. With this I cast sideways, while wading up the long leafy tunnel beside water rushing past and over rock, myself standing in a light both translucent and green, intent and happy, my eyes watching for the least break in the dark flow where a fish had risen, my ears attuned to the ousel notes of running water. I used that little rod later, as I shall describe, in Canada, in the Hebrides and in Florida; it rests in my rod-stand today, more than a quarter of a century after I bought it.

· · · · ·

I Visit a Fish Farm, and Meet Poachers

When the autumnal rains at the beginning of my second year at Shallowford darkened the valley, and made sodden the meadows of the deer park; when the leaves of valley trees were whirled away, to join others carried down by every hillside runner and meadow drain to the river swollen and gleaming palely under sunless skies, I ceased feeding what were now called the tame fish in their various pools. The loss of summer was not easy to bear, so one morning, having finished a book, I set out to explore down-stream. I walked beside a long and deep pool held back by the weir of the estate sawmills, which were worked by a water-wheel fed by a leat leading water away from the weir. Below the weir I watched a salmon jumping into yellow cascading water. After several jumps it hung by its paired fins to one of the mossy stones which made a rough buttress below the sill. Whether these steps had been built there for the fish to ascend by, I did not know; I doubted it, for when it was built, the fishing in the river, so high up, was not considered to be of value, according to a brother of the Lord of All, a writer who had, some years previously, helped me in my literary career.

There was an old fender beside the weir, on the bank opposite the leat, reached by a path through the wood on the hill slope above; I had been there often, scheming how I could open the fender. It was set in a frame of oak, a door made to be lifted, for water to shoot away under and down a stone-paved spillway. Obviously a fish-pass, it was now choked by mud on its upper side. I could not shift it; levering sticks broke off. It had been stuck there for years. Later, I opened it with my iron bar.

I explored farther down the river. A mile or two below the sawmills was a terrifying obstacle. Here, to lead water

I Visit a Fish Farm, and Meet Poachers

to a grist mill, a dam had been built nearly eight feet high on solid rock. Salmon, both rusty-red and bronze, were trying to jump up the impossible cliff face, with dozens of smaller sea-trout. Salmon, to jump, need to spring out of water. Before springing, the fish has to swim up in full acceleration, in order to continue its spurt in air. Below this weir was no pool out of which to swim. Water thundered over the sill, bashing itself and all with it on rock whose stratum lay jagged across the river. Every fish, as I watched, fell back as though hurt. Some were carried away belly up, each a tragic sight as I thought of the homing fish come from the security of the sea not for themselves, not for personal profit (for a salmon did not feed in fresh water) but to serve its race. I began to see these fish as noble and tragic creatures, like soldiers in battle, in the test to destruction, upheld only by tenuous dream, which was honour.

I went home, and returned with a crowbar, hiding it under my coat, lest the miller across the river see what I intended to do. Fitting the angled end into the rusted iron holes by which the fender was made to be lifted, with a ratchet to hold it up at various heights, I heaved and jerked and bore down with my eleven-stone weight until I felt the sodden mass of the two-inch oaken door beginning to shift. Under its base a jet of muddy water hissed. Leaves and black twigs gushed through. It was plain that if I slipped from the oak plank crossing the spillway I would be swept into the river by the jets now shooting under me. Inch by inch the tottery oaken door came up. I was determined to lift its base clear of the coloured race now passing with many roars just under the clammer plank on which I stood. It took most of my energy to lift the base of the

I Visit a Fish Farm, and Meet Poachers

fender clear of water, and then I tried to work the rusty ratchet into its slot, but could not manage it. What would happen if the fender dropped suddenly? Would it burst from its frame, and carry all away, myself included?

Sweating, with thudding heart, I tried to work the fender one inch higher, while calculating the weight of the water passing beneath me. The spillway was five feet wide; the water-level in the pool behind the fender seven feet above the spillway floor. If the frame gave, how many cubic yards of water, each weighing a ton, would rush underneath me every second, at the speed of a trotting horse?

To my relief I found that I could rest; the pressure of water kept the fender from dropping. I tried again. The clammer plank held, so did my nailed shoes, as jerk by jerk I got the fender up, clear of the rush of water, and held by the ratchet. I went to look at the weir, to see that no more salmon were beating themselves to death there. They had found the main thrust of water up the spillway.

During November the rains abated, but December of that year was the oddest month. The nights might have been of April and May, but the days! The rainstorms began on the second of the month, and fell almost continuously during daylight, except during two bright mornings. The river swelled and spread, a turgid brown, into the verges of the meadows. One night I saw in the headlights of my motor two otters on the road, crossing to rabbit buries in the hillside above the deer park. Fishing for them in such water was impossible; they were probably after rabbits.

When the level fell, a jetsam of twigs, leaves, a dead hen, an occasional empty tin or corked medicine bottle lay on the grass yards away from the alders. The water cleared, but the main flow was still heavy. The river, fed by tribu-

63

tary springs and runners, kept a steady level. New sandy beaches lay on the deer park grass, with edgings of twigs and leaves scratched over by pheasants seeking acorns. More rain fell. The sand bars were re-made by another and greater spate many yards above the banks. Over the moor the sky was leaden. Tree trunks rode down, damming the arches of bridges. Some tipped over Sawmills Weir, scaring salmon lying in the eddies below. When the water again fined down the river was still in high spate. In one place, some miles below my beat, under a weir near the junction pool of the river with another, the water was purple-brown with the mass of fish resting there. Each fish in the comparative calm of the backwash appeared to await its turn to bore up against the white thunder racing down the sloping weir-face. I scared away a starved-looking heron every time I went there.

One fish after another, sometimes two and three together, leapt up and fell aslant and quivered, so it seemed, within the rushing glide of solid water. Many were caught by undulating waves at the leap, flung over backwards, swept away. These were, possibly, newcomers, testing the power and direction of the various streams or bores which made up the thundering water-weights.

Those fish which had determined to go up and over gripped the water they pierced at the end of their leaps and began to swim. They were discernible as vibrating shapes moving very slowly. Often the water-weight was too heavy. After a period varying between five and ten seconds they turned on their sides, and were hurled among the broken wave-masses below. Many of these fish were pink, with yellow heads and elongated jaws, the spawning dress of the 'soldier', the young male salmon. Among them were sea-trout, brown-spotted mother of pearl. A few fish were bronze-brown, the females. Of some the skin of their lower jaws was worn away, revealing bone. They appeared to be enfeebled by the long stay, without food, in fresh water. There was no dash in their jumping.

During a sunlit moment I saw a silver flash in the torrent and a clear-run salmon leapt six feet out of the white upsurge, and fell with a splash into the swift glide of water. It went up steadily, and I thought as I counted the seconds that it would never reach the sill of the weir. Now it seemed to be motionless, its back fin cutting the water with lines of spray, with back-flung water drips. Then it shot forward. A little later it leapt in the pool above, blue-green and white curve, an impulse of joy in life which was passed to me. This was one of the fish called green-backs, which came into fresh water in winter, clean-run fish.

By opening the fender at Steep Weir I had annoyed certain salmon poachers, who came from the town with gaffs, twisted brass nooses on poles, and even dung-forks. Four of them eyed me sullenly as I arrived by the fender, which I found closed on my second visit. These men were out of work, through no fault of their own: at that time two million in Britain were permanently without jobs. I talked with some of them, who had fought in the war. I said that the flesh of the purple and brown fish in the river was poor: that some were kelts, which needed to clean themselves in the sea. They were not good to eat.

'But what about they green-backs? They'm clane enough! They'm what you water-whipping gentry call clean-run. The lice be still upon 'm! They green-backs kick up the eggs already laid, and put down their own, for what purpose? Shall I tell 'ee? For to breed more green-backs, to do the same thing, and kick up more eggs, and take their place, until all you rod-and-line men will have is green-backs to catch by whippin' water in winter. Then where's your spring sport, with a nice packet o' sandwiches and a nip o' whiskey? Can yew answer me that, tho'?'

I could not; so I gave them a few shillings each for this information, saying that I was a writer, and paid for information; and at least they had not condemned me to a watery death when I had re-opened the fender. I gave them a lift back to the town, where they entered a butcher's shop to buy pork chops, with which they set off for their homes, seeming to be as pleased as I was.

Dark Months

During winter the sun did not shine into the lower rooms of our cottage, for upon the hill opposite was a plantation whose trees would not be ready for felling for some years. The sun rose behind a higher hill farther east, and the low curve of winter brought its rim below the pines and spruces, which shadowed the hamlet. Rime lay on our two lawns, each with its yew-tree, and was hardly melted when frore mists crept over them again, and the day once more was darkening.

In the upper rooms the sun did blink for a while, as it rolled among the treetops with an illusion of warmth. The fireplace in my study over the dining-room was another early Victorian shell of cast iron, warming the chimney. One day, to escape wintry thoughts, I set out to walk down the valley to the estuary and the sea.

Companioned by dog and blackthorn thumb-stick, I followed the valley road and came to where the stream joined its elder brother; and onwards past widening meadows, I arrived at the Junction Pool, where the waters of west Exmoor flowing south joined those of cousin Taw flowing west from Dartmoor. I walked down this ultimate valley, which I had known years before, when following the hounds for my book on the otter. In those days many of the Cheriton subscribers used to walk on the railway line, which often ran beside the river: the Gentleman's River, it was called, for there were inns convenient for midday stops along its serpentining length.

Again I walked on the line, hopping from sleeper to sleeper, before taking to the road for swifter progress. It was cold that January day, and I was glad of an inn; and abandoning the idea to walk all the way, I caught a westward bound train to the town, and alighting at one station beyond, followed the sheep-path on the banks of the pill —the Anglo-Saxon name still in use for the creek—which led to the estuary.

The tide was lapsing, the sandbanks were covered with a brittle crust of ice. North-east wind whipped the water. The shepherd returning across the saltings walked bent-knee'd, collar up, head down, sack on shoulders, hands in pockets, nose-tip red. Curled breast feathers of gulls were lightly fixed on the glazing mud, prickled with glasswort, whence the sea had ebbed.

Over the moor the sky had a hard grey dullness, as of snow withheld. To the south lay the Burrows, piled by the prevailing ocean winds of centuries. It was said that these sands beyond the shores of the estuary covered an oak forest. Bones of moose, elk and other animals, including the jaw of a sabre-toothed tiger, had been found across the channel, in clay studded with carbonized wood still visible at low spring tides. It was cold on the shore. Far away, a chevron descended and assumed the shape of two eyebrows: the white-fronted geese had come down before the Arctic blasts. A local naturalist I had met in the village told me that a snowy owl had been seen quartering the marsh in daylight.

Dark Months

A year or two before, a Greenland falcon had hunted over the flats behind the sandhills during that hard winter. It had stooped on duck from its mile-high pitch, the noise of the wind in its barbed wings being audible half a mile away. Later it was trapped in an illegal pole-trap, there still being at that time a few older sportsmen of the stuffed glass-case school in the district. The fly-tying taxidermist in the town had shown the bird in his window for some weeks. Controlled anger showed in his brown eyes that such a rare bird had been killed, and so barbarously; but to his credit he did not criticize his patron who had brought it in to be stuffed and mounted.

Walking on the shingle by the lighthouse I watched four porpoises which had come up with the flowing tide, and were now returning with the lapse. I imagined that they had followed a run of greenback salmon, and now were playing. They drove through the junction of the Two Rivers' tides marked by the string of dirty foam made by the press of currents in mid-channel. Now and again a porpoise would curve out of the water, to fall back bottle-head first, leaving a boil where it had disappeared.

The porpoises, which may have been two pairs, rolled their merry way down the fairway towards the bar and the open sea. They bobbed and sported, their feeding done; but they had been observed when they came in with the tide, and some other predatory mammals were interested in their return.

The tide was going out fast; it was almost time of the new moon, when the springs, having pressed up to their limit in the arms of the land, would retreat far from the shore. Over the fairway buoys, now leaning westward, water broke in plumes. Wind gave another half-knot to the tide-lapse. At five knots the water jostled back to ocean. I saw the black and immature whales blowing spray from their spiracles. They turned to swim on their backs. Sometimes they leapt from the water and fell back with crashings. Did they, like salmon, have itching parasites? The animals moved so swiftly that an irregular trail of foam was left behind them for half a mile.

Below the pool a boat put out. Two men rowed strongly. The porpoises sported towards the boat. Did they see, with eyes scarcely larger than those of moles, their enemies? A third man in the bows of the boat raised a gun, took aim and fired. One of the sea-hogs appeared to twist backwards as it came out of the water. The other three dived deep, reappearing nearly two hundred yards away for the least respiration, then down at once. I did not see the fourth porpoise again.

During that cold spell, on my walks by the river, I was able to observe the several distinct changes of the partial freezing of a rapid stream.

At the beginning of the period any stone or stick or root or fern which was sprayed or regularly wetted near a fall or other obstruction became coated with ice. Brambles which during the summer had pushed through the alders to find rootage for their young green tips, and had found instead the surface of water, became clubbed with ice. This ice, as in the case of ferns and roots, was made of innumerable layers of thin water. The club of ice on the bramble became slowly heavier; the bramble grew backwards and forwards less quickly from its spring of alder branches, until the weight of ice extended it diagonally down-stream.

Dark Months

Water piled up against the moored ice-bottle, which lost its slender neck and became thickened as though by an inexperienced glass-blower. All living things feel some sort of pain; and if the burden of ice did not tear away the bramble from its bush, or a thaw release it from torture, next spring it would hang there red and coarse, finally to wither and die.

The frost held. Brittle plates of ice formed across still water by the sides of runs and eddies. Icicles, at that time still called cockabells by some Devon children, hung under the falls where before water had trickled slowly. Ice thus sealed the trickling places. The water trickled elsewhere, making new cockabells. Rocks and obstacles were thickened by ice, and gradually the water-level in the river bed was raised. Pieces of ice were levered up, and broke away and were carried down to the next eddy where they lodged or rode slowly until welded into packs of ice by the banks.

I noticed that the slow solidification of eddies and still stretches by the shallows narrowed the waterway and caused the runs to move faster, creating thereby other reactions or eddies or resistance; for moving water is governed by the same laws which govern all the movement called life. Life is action, movement, progress as well as reaction, resistance, conservance; but action, movement, progress are alone of the Spirit which giveth life, as the biblical poet perceived.

The plates of ice holding frost strove to convert running water, which lagged thereby and weakened in its purpose for life. Grasses and rushes helped to hold the ice. Towards midday the sun in a clear sky subdued the arrogance of rime, melting first the hoofmarks of cattle and wild deer which wandered along the banks. Above the fall the water raised by the dam of ice suddenly pressed a way through. Dead leaves churned with sand in the pool below. Soon the warning noises ran down with the fuller stream: ice crackling and whimpering, some of it breaking away to ride down tilting and heaving. The shadowed piers of Humpy Bridge below held the floes, which frost instantly began to work upon, sealing them to the stonework.

In the afternoon when I went out to look again the sun was behind the trees, the grass drooped once more as the rime settled. Up above by the beech tree, the weir was thicker with ice. Thin layers of water ran over that ice, annealing it. Thus the war went on, heat against cold, life against death. If there were salmon in the pool below they were scarcely stirred by the greater flow; cold numbed them, quelling their desire to reach the redds, the spawning pits in the gravel beds, where eggs and milt were shed.

At night, as I walked to post letters in the box upon the main road half a mile away, the Dog Star was green above the south-eastern horizon. It was freezing hard. All the usual water-sounds were dulled, except by the falls. A mist moved upon the starlit face of the waters, becoming denser and pressing nearer the surface as midnight boomed from some cottage wireless set. Returning over the road bridge, by the stark sycamore tree, I looked down into the water. My ear-tips were smarting, and the breath on my moustache was rime as I peered over the cold stone, while down below it seemed that the mist had joined with the slush dragging slower in the faint-hearted river. The falls above still roared, but with lessening power: and while I peered, the splayed glittering of the Dog Star on the surface was gone. Ice lay across the pool, from bank to bank.

As I have said, the winter sun did not reach over the trees of the plantations on the hill to the south, so our lower rooms remained dull all day. I made myself walk every afternoon, but it was not easy to struggle against a set desire to continue living in an imaginary world built on feelings, and expressed only in words upon paper. The copper oil-lamp was lit early, beech logs burned in the open hearth, shutters closed against the ruinous day.

Thus the year's dead end. When ice and frost had gone, and the river below Humpy Bridge was running cloudy with snow water, I began to feed the trout again, except on those days when too heavy a volume of water was rushing down. To my joy, they were still there. Winter spates had piled heavy masses of sticks and branches against the cutwaters of the bridge. One morning I returned for my waders, canvas brogues and a rope, and walked into the river, meaning to clear them.

The waders came only to the tops of my thighs; and going forward on tip-toe, I slipped and in a moment the waders were filled, and I was dragged down. It was a strange slow feeling, to be carried away and to see the lime stalactites under the arch above me, the old mossy nest of the dipper on the stone shoulder of the arch. Then I was being spun top-wise down the waterfall into the pool below. Quite calmly I wondered if I should be drowned. The calmness went as I swallowed a mouthful of water, helplessly moving towards the tail of the pool, my ballooning legs above me, my head being pressed under water. I felt as a salmon must feel, held by the tail upstream, while the water opened its gill-covers and drowned it. But the rocking water bumped me upon the line of heavy stones I had laid in summer to deepen the pool. There I held, swinging round in the current. I got out but fell over on the bank, numbed by cold. Lying on my back, I managed to lift up my feet, and hold them there while the water ran out from monstrous pellicle-waders. Then I could get up, legs and hands aching almost violently.

Feeling that I needed to test my will, I returned to the obstruction lodged against the piers, this time without foolish waders, and lugged at a three-hundredweight oak branch. My heart pounded; blackness rushed in my ears and eyes; so I waited, then pulled myself out on the bank. It was a shameful and exasperating feeling, to be so unfit, so I went in once more, made fast the rope, and returned home to change my clothes, warm with having satisfied my inner self, animated by a stinging glow.

Fishing for trout began with March; but the native or wild trout were still thin from winter starvation, their short guts filled with small stones and specks of stick which they had grubbed up from the river-bed, being the houses of the larvae of black gnat and caddis fly. Considering myself to be 'a dry-fly purist', I was content to wait until at least mid-April, when the native brownies would be in condition, and water-sparkles reflect the life of sun and sky. When sandpipers, back from Africa, ran lightly, and fluttered briefly as though loath to leave their images where the meadow grass verged upon the water, then was the time to throw my hackle fly.

Meanwhile it was my pleasure to feed the tame fish, as the family spoke of them. Daily, usually at noon, I went to

Dark Months

Humpy Bridge. The three big fellows had by now left the pool below. Two of them had got so far as the Fireplay. Many of the two-year-olds, now getting on for three years, remained. As soon as the figure of my head and shoulders appeared above, they swam up from the bottom to take up position in the stream straking the surface of the pool below the three archways. These streams straggled out until they slowed to quiet swirlings, like bubbled query marks at the tail of the pool, where my barrage of heavy stones had withstood the winter.

At the first shower the Loch Levens broke surface, showing their black spots. To my delight, some of the brown spots had turned red, from feeding on flies and nymphs. And as I stood there, again I heard the mysterious drumming of the lesser spotted woodpecker coming across the park. How did it make that sound?

Every morning, some time before I left the cottage, I damped the day's food for the tame trout. It was contained in a large toffee tin I had picked out of the river after a spate. With a spoon flick I cast some on the water. At once green and yellow flanks were curving, tails breaking out; scores of curves were cut across one another. Some fish jumped out in their eagerness. It was a fine sight; they were as large as herrings, and at times as close as herrings in a net.

Above the bridge, other fish were waiting. I could see them, head to stream, pressed down against the gravel, some behind stones. Among them a few wild brown trout and salmon parr. At the first spoonful more fish raced down from the run at the bend of the river above where now, since 'them stinking violets' were in bloom, several hunters belonging to the Young Lord were out to grass, from Leicestershire at the end of the fox-hunting season.

Just as a huntsman knows every hound in his pack, by both tongue and look, as a shepherd knows his ewes, so I came to know every fish in the clear water above the bridge. Most conspicuous was an old brownie, which when first I had seen him, during the previous year had been big-headed, dark and thin. I guessed his weight to be a pound, his age to be nine or ten years. A trout is in its prime between three and a half and four years. This old creature, being slow, could not compete for flies and nymphs with the younger, more lively fish. He was probably an occasional cannibal, past spawning. Nor was he in the least sociable—at first. When the new fish had jumped about for food, he had waggled his tail and moved into the obscurity of mud under the floating alder roots by the bank.

He was there after the winter, occasionally visible during the spring showers of food, but remaining aloof; but not so sullenly as before. Sometimes he would cruise among the lively shoal, swish his tail as though excited by his daring, and then drift back to his hide again. Perhaps he had been hooked a year or two before, and had not forgotten it. I hoped he would take the food, and change his sombre coat into one of greenish-blue, like the native fish that were taking the food.

I bought an eel-trap, from an advertisement in *The Fishing Gazette*. Having been baited with head, feet and entrails of a hen, it was dropped on a rope by some alder roots in the bank above the bridge. The next day the dour old fish was missing, and I imagined he had been taken by an otter which had travelled up the river the night before.

Dark Months

The water-beast's claw-marks were to be seen, where it had climbed out below the first waterfall, by the tall beech trees. Thence it had run some way along a path in the meadow parallel to the bank. This was a well-worn otter path. It ended by an ant-hill, the grass of which had been killed during the previous summer by otters' urine. During the winter, when the otters kept to the lower reaches of the river, perhaps hunting salmon in the big pools, the ant-hill never showed the marks of spraints; and by March it was the greenest thing in the deer park, the numerous eel-bones upon and around it hidden in rank grass. And the day the old trout was missed, fresh, dark-green spraints lay on the ant-hill, where an otter had touched the night before.

But when I hauled in my eel-trap, a cylinder of gal-vanized wire netting, and lifted it out, dripping with weed, I saw a dark-brown fish flapping within. It was the old brownie. Five smaller trout were with him. The bait was uneaten.

The head of the trap, which had lain upstream, was clogged with weed. I wondered if the trout had swum up the narrow one-way funnel at the rear of the trap, not for food, but for shelter.

Lugging the trap well back from the bank, I opened the door in the top, and tipped the cylinder for the fish to slither out. The small trout jumped about, but the old fellow, whose head and jaws suggested a crocodile, began to writhe through the grasses to the river. As he seemed to need no help, I let him continue until his nose stuck in some soft mud made by the feet of cattle. Then, having wetted my hand, I eased him into the water. He swam forward, his snout tipped with mud. Having put back the other fish, I ran up to the parapet of the bridge, to watch what the big fish would do. He was lying on the gravel.

A spoonful of food, and at once the water was rocking; jaws snapping, tails swishing through the broken surface. To my surprise the old trout, hitherto so sluggish and suspicious, was quicker than the others. He raised a wave as he came downstream, he made a slashing rise as he leapt to take a piece of floating food before the opening mouth of a Loch Leven. I threw in more food. He cut and swirled after it. The mud was still on his snout. He behaved as a dog behaves when released from its mournful wait at the end of a chain; or an innocent man reprieved from death, when the shock is passing away.

Whether or not the fish was a mindless creature of 'automatic reflex actions', I saw a fish behaving as I would have behaved had I been that fish. And from that moment he ceased to be shy of human presence on the bridge. He came down with the others when he saw my figure, to await food. He had no feeling for me, as a person (I think); and I wondered if what he saw of me on land was different from his underwater vision of the figure on the bridge. Would he not be short-sighted on land, with the lens of each eye adjusted to subaqueous vision?

I re-baited the trap with rabbits' pots; and when I hauled it out the next day from the pool below the bridge, the old trout was again inside. I tipped him once more upon the grass, in the same place, and helped him to wriggle back into the water above the bridge. Back in the water, he behaved like a clown, skittering about among the fish waiting for the food showers.

As summer advanced more fish joined that little watery Band of Hope, including salmon parr and one or two small peal (sea-trout) which, escaping the thirty-six nets working in the estuary from two hours before to two hours after every low tide, ran up from the sea in the silver sea-dresses which covered the spots of their river-coats.

How well-behaved they were! Each fish knew its place, maintaining order of precedence, the bold reformed Clown at their head, where he could get (theoretically) the pick of each cast. Sometimes I threw short, and he came down speedily to claim his rights. He had by now lost his dark colour; his flanks were pale gold, the dull maroon pennant, or adipose fin, bore a bright vermilion spot. His blue-black head had changed to brown, and no longer looked too big. He lay beside fingerling trout, rejuvenated and benevolent.

The Judge's Warning

When eyed ova of salmon from the Tay arrived, early in another year, I put them in a tray within the surface well that fed, by gravitation, the cistern for bath-water up near the kitchen ceiling, before digging a pit at the end of the garden, in which to rear the fry. The pond would be fed by water from the runner, or little brook, in the bottom of the coombe, which was marshy.

I set about this job with pick, cutting spade and long-handled Devon shovel. The going was hard. I was not used to labouring work; I had never acquired the slow rhythm of the body, the patience of manual work, the tortoise contentment of work being done, day after day, steadily and contentedly, I was the hare; I tore into the work with all my nervous mental energy, no happy substitute for the slower, enduring rhythm of the labourer who digs with skill. The soil in the marsh at the bottom of the garden was yellow clay. Soon the pick was useless: so was the man at the end of the sticky handle, needing more energy to pull it out than to drive it in—for what? It was useless. So I started afresh, trying to work as when a child I had seen navvies working, with pail of water, wooden spade-cleaner stuck in strap hitching corduroy trousers above ankles, and a flagon bottle of ale. After each cut, thrust and lift of spade, the chunk having dropped off the steel, the navvy dipped his spade in the pail to lubricate it for the next cut and lift. Thus a pipe-trench, or a grave, was dug out exactly, almost mathematically, with smooth sides without fault.

But good intentions are no substitute for good habits. My ill-adjusted mood was too impatient. I tore into the work, helped by my man who, throughout the sweat and puff, talked of the works of Tolstoi, Shelley and Shakespeare. Soon we were covered by clay marn, our hands, hair, shovel handles, boots, clothes, all indeed except our mouths and eyes. It was Ypres again, but without the lost horizon. Somehow or other, in two days, we were six feet down, standing in puddled ochre to our knees, holding in our fin-like hands kitchen buckets and children's seaside pails. A plunge into the river soon washed away the clay from my clothes and person, leaving after my exit from the stream a yellow stain moving down. It was fun by this time.

The digging of the leat from the runner under the hedge, to lead water to the pond, was a pleasant job, to the accompaniment of theories about Dostoievsky, Henry Fielding and Henri Barbusse. By this time I knew enough to dig the channel before making a dam in the runner, by which to raise the water-level. It was done by the time my helper and I had got back to Tolstoi. We made screens of perforated zinc held within rectangular wooden frames, afterwards painting them with bituminous black paint against fungus growths and the oxidization of the zinc with consequent poisoning of water. A grill of iron bars, borrowed from the kitchen stove, was put in front of the first screen inside the fender, or penstock, which controlled the volume of water flowing into the leat, to collect leaves and sticks which otherwise would choke the screen. The leaves etc. must, of course, be cleared daily.

The screen's purpose was to keep eels and other preying creatures from entering the flume, or stream flowing down the leat. Another screen was placed below the outfall of the pond, to stop eels and mullheads working up into the fry nursery. The job being done, and again yellow with glutinous clay, I swam about in the river, thus washing my clothes and hands and hair, before motoring to the fish farm, returning with 250 yearlings which were duly introduced into their new home.

Meanwhile the salmon eggs were in the well; it would be some time before I would see salmon parr in my neat new pond, at the bottom of which an old pair of my boots were stuck, having been abandoned there owing to suction. They would collect algae, and feed water-snails. So I thought to use the pond for trout, while the salmon fry were growing up in the leat—which would have more screens to protect them. For shade in future seasons, Canadian willow slips were stuck a yard back from the banks. A wire-net fence was also needed, but literary work had to be done, so with reluctance I went back to my study, gradually to lose the free feeling of the body working in the elements. I became broody, and soon was as reluctant to leave the desk as I had been to leave the yellow clay pit.

One evening I broke my routine, a bad one of writing all day and often late into the night, and visited The Fisherman's Arms. In the bar I renewed acquaintance with an old sportsman who stayed there for a fortnight every year. I

The Judge's Warning

told him of my various plans to alter the character of my fishery: how I was going to make dams in the river, if possible of limestone, plant weeds to give holding to natural fish-food, trap eels and improve the breed of salmon by releasing Tay smolts, in due course, into the river.

My acquaintance was a retired judge. At first he said nothing; then having ordered two hot Irish whiskies, with lemon, brown sugar and water, he remarked, 'That is most interesting. By the way, I did not kill any of your Loch Leven fish last season, but I heard about them.' Slowly he filled a well-coloured meerschaum pipe, lit the tobacco, took a few pulls to get it going and closed the silver lid. 'Yes, most interesting.' He was over eighty, lean, fit and philosophical. We met when following otter-hounds in the past, and some things he had told me then had gone into *Tarka*. Now he gave me the following story, while from the next room came the knock and soft clatter of wood, as some of the moormen played their nightly table-skittles by the light of an oil lamp on the wall.

'What you tell me about your plans reminds me of the Worcestershire ironmaster who, on buying a property, set about improving on nature. Man has always striven to do that, of course, and not always with success. But please do not deduce, from what I am going to say, that I think your plans are a prelude to disaster.'

He sipped his hot drink, the continued in his carefully modulated tones. 'You know Plunkett Greene's *Where the Bright Waters Meet*, of course? No? I must lend you my copy, if you care to borrow it. The book is a classic, charming, oh delightful! Plunkett Greene rented some water near Whitchurch in Hampshire, a small brook where trout of two and three and four pounds were common. It was a chalk stream, of course. After a while he introduced fish from a hatchery, and how the older native fish slowly starved, grew thin and black, and probably blind, until the water was spoiled, makes doleful reading. But let me say again, do not think that I am implying a like fate for your fish. Now for the ironmaster's story—

'This rich man, on buying a property, with the keenness of new proprietorship, the new broom, you know, wanted, among other things, a perfect fishery. He began by systematically ridding his river of vermin. He planned it on business lines, step by step. His water-bailiffs trapped otters, as the biggest enemies. When this had been achieved, the river suffered a plague of eels. These he removed by means of hundreds of baited traps, no doubt bought by the gross at a considerable trade discount. After a season the bed of his river was overpopulated by innumerable mullheads, or miller's thumbs. These fish, miscalled loach by some writers, are squat, wide-mouthed, bull-headed and about two inches long. Previous to the mass withdrawal of eels the mullheads had lived under stones, watching for food moving past their hovers.

'Now, with no natural enemies except the trout, they multiplied exceedingly. They covered the river-bed, eating not only all the trout food, but the eggs of trout as they were laid in October and November, and what fry survived to hatch in February and March.

'During the spring and early summer, all the squire had in his river was a plague of mullheads, and a few enormous bottom-feeding trout. These monsters had no progeny; and in the course of time, all the mullheads were eaten up. The trout were by then too old to spawn. Black, gaunt

The Judge's Warning

wrecks lay in the water, gradually becoming fungoid; and then extinct. Shall we fill up our glasses?'

We did so, and the story proceeded.

'The squire had interests in industrial milling at the port of Liverpool, using the hard wheat of Canada; his grandfather had owned a water-mill in East Anglia. One day, examining a very rare fish netted in his river, an albino fish, the very last of its race, he realized how the name *Miller's thumb* had come into the language. Obviously it was connected with the water-mills, which used to grind corn into flour. He remembered his grandfather's mill-pond, which had always been full of excellent fish, unlike his own river, which now, after the removal of the white freak, was empty of everything except water.

'His interest, casual as it was, in the origin of the name *Miller's thumb*, was the start of the squire's new lease of life; for realizing that he had ruined his river, he had fallen into a state of melancholy and reflection. He ate little, and spent many hours alone in his library, burning the midnight oil, poring over old books on the subject of rivers, mills, corn and the Black Death.'

'In other words, he had become that object of complete decadence, a literary gent,' I said.

'I would not go so far as to say that to the author of *Tarka*,' replied the old gentleman, with a smile. 'One night, opening his father's Bible box, he found an old letter, in faded ink, written by his grandmother. In it he read that poor Jno (as his grandmother referred to his grandfather, John) had hit his thumb again, while pecking anew the grooves in his Frenchy-made grit-stone with the peck. Working as usual by tallow dip—no doubt a jug of scrumpy cider beside him in the room draped in white from the flour dust upon innumerable cobwebs—Jno had mistaken the shadow for the substance, and struck the thumb of his left hand, already splayed by so many knocks in the past.

'The letter gave heart to the grandson, now a heavily bearded recluse, alone in his library; and recalling delightful walks by the river with his dear grandpappy, he went down to look at his own stream, once so full of splendid fish, and now a mere water Gomorrah, or, as he put it to himself, a veritable Pillar of Salt. Beside banks overgrown with thorn and bramble, the vegetation of the wilderness, he loitered; and it was there that he had a vision, a veritable Jacob's Ladder, he said later, anent the balance of Nature. He saw life as an entity: one species absorbing another—water and its fluids into algae, algae into daphne and nymph, and so to fry, miller's thumb, eel, heron and otter; and otters occasionally into hounds, whose masters and committee owners are likely to vanish through the new sentiment of the towns, where now Jack is as good as his master.'

Fresh drinks were brought.

'There was yet time to put back the clock; and hurrying home, he wrote to a firm of zoological collectors, ordering great quantities of miller's thumbs, eels, trout, otters, which in due course were turned into the river. Later, he purchased several couple of otter-hounds, with which to breed a pack, to keep down the otters. These beasts he regularly hunted. Thus the *status quo* was restored, and he, as patron, occasionally squeezed himself in between the balance, and with rod and line passed many a relaxing hour in and beside the water. Now it will give me great pleasure if you will drink a night-cap with me, for I must not keep you any

The Judge's Warning

longer; and being an old man, I find the air of the moor makes me sleepy after nine o'clock.'

This graceful hint was followed by a finger lifted towards the waiter; and having toasted one another, we said good night, and I drove away over the narrow lanes, twisting as they rose and fell, back to my valley, the moon lighting my way. When I stopped, I heard the churring of evejars; and arising with the warm airs, the remote noises of water running everywhere down from the heathery commons.

It was one of those nights when the heart is lifted above the cares of ordinary living, and one feels that stones, trees, stars and all so-called inanimate life have their own spiritual existence. Walking up the garden path, I passed beside the apple trees, and stopped to receive their feeling. The first flakes of the blossom were lying upon the soil, the dew condensing on the white petals. So peaceful was it that I stood under a tree, resting myself in the night. Something glistened with faint phosphorescence below me. I switched on my torch, and saw that many worms had moved up their galleries from the lower earth, and were putting out their heads to feel the night air. They seemed to be listening—not with ears, but with their entire bodies, which were sensitive to all ground vibrations. Sitting upon the earth, I watched worm after worm beginning to move out of its tunnel, and with eager pointed head to search for petals. When one was found, it was taken into the worm's mouth and the worm withdrew all but its head into its tunnel, to leave the petal outside the hole and move out again in another direction, casting about until it found another flake. This, too, was drawn back to the tunnel entrance, and left there, while the search went on as before.

The Judge's Warning

Crouching against the tree trunk, I watched lobworms moving in all directions, seeking the finest food of the year—the spring feast of apple blossom. Each worm had its tail in its hole, ready at the least earth-tremor to pull itself back in one swift movement which brought all but the head into the hole. Then, after a second gathering of itself, it withdrew the head to safety.

When a worm had, and so carefully, gathered about a dozen petals, it picked them up in its mouth and then went down into the darkness to eat them. Thus the night-wanderer turned blossom into finest soil, or humus, which fed the rootlets of the tree once more. It was a soil-maker; its galleries and tunnels acted as drains to the top soil. It seemed to me, as I sat there, that worms were priests of the soil, the great mother which gave all life.

That night as I lay in bed, between waking and sleeping, a rare feeling of being suspended in timeless space, the notes of a flute overlay the water-sounds from the runner at the end of the marsh. I was not sure whether the notes were in my head, or upon the air; they were part of my happiness, true relaxation. I thought distantly of otters, and then that what had already happened, if it was so, could not be helped.

In the morning the yellow clay of the pond's surround was puddled everywhere by five-toed seals, with here and there a fish scale. Three trout were left in my pond. Otters had collected some of the royalties from *Tarka*.

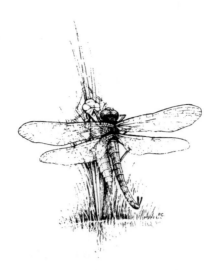

I Make a Hatchery

As the fishmaster had told me, Tay fish were hog-backed; salmon of the western rivers were long and thin by comparison. In imagination I saw a thick-set grilse in front of every concrete dam, as well as in the natural pools. Perhaps if I could get the fry to feed on flies, I might breed a run of fish to take the dry fly, as clean-run salmon did in the rivers of Newfoundland.

I wanted to have a hatchery on my dining-room table, and had bought for this purpose some zinc trays, painted black, from the fish farm. Smaller trays, but perforated, fitted into the outer trays.

Now for the stream of water.

My idea was to bore a small hole in the pipe bringing water to the cottage by gravitation from the well on higher ground, first having plugged the inlet at the well. The pipe had a bore of one and a half inches. The next thing was to tap, i.e. turn, a thread in the hole, to take a small brass cock stolen from my elder son's stationary steam-engine. By fitting a rubber tube to the cock, a jet of water could be led into the glass aquarium at one end of the table, which was long and heavy and dark, made of oak, and coming originally from some farm kitchen or

I Make a Hatchery

servants' hall. It had a removable top two inches thick, which required two men to lift it off its frame.

The aquarium was already the home of a goldfish, some scavenging snails, a few freshwater shrimps and the shucks of the Large Stone Creeper. The insects once inhabiting these shucks had, almost as soon as they found themselves in the aquarium, left on wings, and flown back to the river.

The overflow from the aquarium was to be led by way of a pipe into the first tray, three inches below the water-level in the glass tank. A terrace of trays, stepped down, would receive the water by gravitation; the outfall from the last tray, by way of a rubber pipe tied to one leg of the table, passed through a hole in the floor. No damage could be done there, as the joists, which rested on earth, were already rotten. Indeed, during a party one night, some of the twenty guests sitting at table had gone through the floor.

Everything having been fixed upon the table according to plan, I removed the plug from the intake pipe in the well, turned on the brass cock, and watched with satisfaction a hard jet of water playing into the aquarium and stirring up the goldfish. The jet drove down with a plume of bubbles, putting oxygen into the water. The goldfish began to wriggle about in alarm; it was not used to freshets. Amidst star-wort and other green plants arising from the sandy bottom strewn with sea-shells scavenging snails went a-roving.

I went away to wash my hands in the bathroom, and out of the tap came a little fish, which began to wriggle around the basin. I caught it in a tooth glass, and carried it down to the aquarium intending to put it, later on, with other alevins when they had grown to fry size, in the Clay Pit.

I Make a Hatchery

What to do with the goldfish? Carp were vegetable feeders, but they also took small worms at times. They were sluggish fish, and like tench could exist in water that would soon kill a trout, which required much oxygen. So Goldie was put, not without anxiety on the children's part, in the Clay Pit for the time being. 'Goldie will take no harm there.'

'But I saw Old Nog looking there the other morning, as he flew down the valley,' said Goldie's owner.

'Old Nog won't bother about so small a tiddler as this.'

'I don't bestways know 'bout that!'

'Anyway, it's only for a short while.'

The solitary alevin soon became a little fish, a fry in fact. It hung in mid-water while watching for food within the outer curl of bubbles small as seed-pearls. There was food in the water, for sometimes it dashed forward to take some diatomic animal thrown out by the jet. When it was not sleeping, or resting, on the sandy bottom it was watching for animalculae which I could not detect even through a magnifying glass. A salmon's life in torrential water had begun.

One afternoon I had to stop the flow, because the owner of the brass cock was giving a party and wanted to work his steam-engine. So the water was turned off, and the hole plugged with wood. I considered there would be enough oxygen in the aquarium and trays to last for about two and a half hours. The alevins in the trays were half-way to becoming fry.

Deprived of the inverted fountain, life in the aquarium drifted to stillness. Its deeps became stagnant, the only movement being that of snails lumbering among sub-aqueous forests in a green twilight. Occasionally a shrimp,

I Make a Hatchery

holding its smaller mate in its arms and legs, flipped among the shells on the floor.

When I looked next, the fry was lying on its back. Its gill-covers opened spasmodically.

I groped for the dying mite, lifted it in my hands, and hastened to the runner. Leaning down, I held it in water trickling through crooked fingers upon my palm. The body, on its back, idled gently to the current. I waited until I saw the mouth open. There was a convulsive gasp. Stillness. Another gulp, gill-covers opening. It began to sinuate, for a while swimming erratically upside down. Suddenly recovering, it darted away, to hide in a cleft between two fingers. I got a pail, filled it with river water, and put the little fish within.

We had been told when taking the place that the water from the shallow well was not fit for drinking, but for bathing only. We drew drinking water from the hamlet tap down the lane. Obviously the well-water held little oxygen, having seeped from the rock of the hillside. My jet, hissing into the aquarium and tearing the water had scattered small bubbles of air, which had partly dissolved as they rose, putting into the water just enough oxygen to support the life of one small fish.

Down to the Clay Pit I went, with pail, shovel and pan, to clear out yellow batter from its bed, and having cleaned and refitted the screens in the leat, I put the fry into the channel of running water. There was good cover under the stones, which had been brought from the river when the pit had been dug. The alevins from the table hatchery went in next, and Goldie went back among his snails in the aquarium.

Later, when the fry were grown to parr size, I intended

I Make a Hatchery

to put them in the pit. To ensure a food supply there, I swam down into the pool below Humpy Bridge and brought up some waterlogged branches, crawling with larvae; and having cut them into suitable lengths, dropped them in the pit. Then, on my way back to the river for more, I heard the woodpecker drumming, very loud this time, directly overhead in a beech tree. I saw it flying away, too—a sparrow-size bird. But I was no wiser about how it made its vibrant call.

When the grass was high and green, and the willow canopies dappled the shade beneath, I spent many a lazy hour beside the rillet, watching the fry hovering, each in its especial place, just under the surface. The fishlet which had come through the tap was still the largest, an inch long by mid-May. I fed to the fry powdered liver, varied by finely chopped hard-boiled yolk of egg. In the sunshine I could see every spot of black and red, the opening of gill-covers, the balancing of fins: the sudden dash forward to take a midge, the slide back to watching place. Sometimes I dropped in a house-fly, and watched the tiny salmon hurling itself at moving legs and wings, again and again, sending up arcs of miniature drops, as it tugged and shook.

From the pond by day arose olive duns, to hide, curved of back and with whisks upheld, like delicate strange air-craft among the willow leaves.

There they shed their pale water-dresses, and later the dance was on; and after the nuptial flights, another change of dress, to sunset-brown, to lure the spinners, the males, rising and falling above the gleaming surface; and the descent to drop their egg-clusters upon what was to them their home.

In the river the two-year-old salmon parr were turning

into smolts, and dropping down to the sea in their new coats. They skipped about excitedly, all was new to them. Their red and black spottings, as in trout, were covered; they were assuming the silver hues of the sea. One morning in May, very early, drawn by cuckoo and skylark, I got out of bed and went into the park; and I walked down the river, all care and cogitation left behind. The air was fresh, dewy-golden; fish were ringing the pools; nymphs of olive dun and other ephemeral flies rising out of the water.

Some time later I caught an early train at a riverside station to the port; and went with the crew of a salmon boat down the six-mile length of the estuary to the Middle Ridge where other boats were waiting to shoot their draughts into the ebbing tide. The water gliding and swirling seawards was azure-milky with the sky. The men could not yet fish; the strong ebb would drag their nets away. The morning was windless, the low eastern sun revealed clearly the cliffs of Lundy and of Hartland promontory. Distant lines of waves were breaking on the sandbars—the dreaded North and South Tails—where enamelled estuary became enamelled sea, and shared the pulse of ocean.

While I stood among the fishermen, a smolt leapt in the fairway. Did it jump with excitement, coming to the great mother of ancestral memory? Or was it being hunted by the bass which rove those waters, fish of dash and power, spiny of gill-cover and back-fin?

'Ah ha! Gude luck to 'ee, my li'l b'uty!' cried one bulbous-nosed veteran of seventy years to the slender sprite, scarcely so long as his hand. This man, and his forebears for a thousand years or more, had taken his living

94

I Make a Hatchery

from salmon since childhood. I had often observed that those who lived by or got part of their livelihood from hunting usually had some regard for the hunted species during its period of immaturity. The tenderness shown towards chicks and ducklings by the farmer's wife was equalled by the protective respect, and even affection, shown to otters, foxes and deer by those who hunted them when they were mature. Such feeling was, I found, often regarded as hypocritical by some critics who did not know, or understand, the complications of even their own natures. At the same time, the thought of a hunted or trapped or even shot beast can be unbearable if one thinks 'too much upon the event'.

Four days later, feeling myself to be sun, sea, sands and air, I returned to the valley, to find everything as I had left it. Trout were rising; so I decided to go fishing.

Upon the lawn I greased the line of my smallest rod, tied on gut and hackle fly, and brogue'd and wader'd, with sandwiches and beer bottle in its sock, ambled to the river. There the sock, having been wetted, was drawn over the bottle left to stand in the sunshine, to grow cold for the moment of drinking.

My idea was to fish upstream until I reached the best place on my beat, the Fireplay, in about two hours' time. There, sitting on the dry gravel heap, my rod with its aluminium spear screwed into butt standing upright in the brake-ferns beside the pool, fly swinging loose to dry, I would draw the cork, and sip cold prickling light ale made from the finest malting barley grown in England—above Porlock Bay on the north Somerset coast.

Meanwhile no hurry. How pleasant it was, released from scriptorial servitude, to stand on Humpy Bridge while the south wind stroked gently the shining grass. The blades were growing visibly. The temperature was rising. Nymphs of the blue-winged olive were swimming up to the surface. The trout were all in position, hovering in mid-water. There was joy in the feeling of being alive, in the thought of my good fortune, in being a medium of such wonders.

Leaning over the parapet, I saw water, slightly brimming over the bleached edges of the bankside gravel after a shower of rain in the night, a-swirl with rises. The fish were lifting themselves up by their swim-bladders, and taking the nymphs as the pellicles broke, each fish then sinking down into mid-water to watch for the next nymph rising before it. Every trout, in its especial place, had its own window or skylight which it watched. The area of visibility, forward and above it, was limited by the angle of refraction, which meant that all outside a fairly steep slant was blank on the fish's sight. The food-stream moved into its skylight.

There were two stone piers in the river, supporting the three arches of the bridge. Each pier had a cutwater which pointed upstream, to divide the force of flowing water. Well in front of the cutwater there was a rebound, a cushion of water where all that came down in the current was momentarily checked. This cushion was usually the place for a Loch Leven trout when the rise was on. Its weight and shape was balanced in the divided water-thrust; it could stay there with the least effort. Also it could, while waiting there, see any nymph coming down in either division of the stream. When another fish approached that cushy place, it was driven away.

Looking down, I saw the Clown resting upon the

I Make a Hatchery

cushion immediately below me. A small alert trout had taken up position in front of the Clown, in the swifter current. From its stance it could dart forward to left or right, and take the sailing, half-winged flies. This smaller fish was beyond the window of the Clown, which waited below, unconscious of the more energetic rival in front of him.

I stood watching in the warm air come into the valley, and in one minute counted twenty-five bulges in front of me. I could not see the fish above, the water being enamelled by the sky; but the immoderation of the swirls revealed where Loch Levens were feeding, for brown trout rose with less dash, their bulging rises were smaller, quieter. They had accepted the river as it was; the Loch Levens were still displaced fish, stew-minded, crowd-competitive.

Amidst the two sorts of bulging rises were mere flicks. These were the eighteen-month-old salmon parr, which would go down as smolts in a year's time. They dashed up at nymphs, taking where they would; they were irrepressible, to the manner born.

The hatch was increasing; sometimes half a dozen bulges appeared together. The sun moving from south-east to south-south-east, I began to detect upriver fish in outline, at first sensed rather than seen: a faint white line of dorsal fin, a group of spots about an almost imagined shape. Now the eager parr were jumping clear, to fall back in their splashes and skitter away from angry trout into whose windows they had plopped.

There was a salmon lying under the arch below my feet, a fish of possibly eight or nine pounds in weight. It had run up early in the year, in glass-green water. Its pristine enthusiasm was gone. At first it had hovered with the trout, even taking an occasional nymph; now it hid beside the foot of the pier, in shadow. Sometimes, after exercise in the night, it thrust itself under the muddy bankside alder roots.

That fish risked death or wounds from four-tined dung-fork, maggots in gill-rakers, eels eating it alive, fungus growing on a tarnished body bruised under a waterfall, until released by the autumn rains; when, if it survived all hazards, it would spawn, an action followed by exhaustion and death, if it were male.

As I lounged there, I saw the salmon move forward to the sterling of the pier below me. Had it felt the buoyancy of water? Had the hatch of fly lured it from its hide under the arch? There it lay, immediately below the skin of the surface, like a trout, sometimes showing a wetness of back and curve of tail as it hovered there. Trout of all sizes were in front of, beside and behind the salmon, each at its station, each happily wimpling in the upper water.

I lolled there while the sun passed the meridian; and all the afternoon, brogues and waders kicked off, I lay on the bank below, near the alder where the lesser spotted wood-pecker had returned to its nesting hole. I watched a crimson dragonfly nymph which had crawled from the water to cling and petrify in its desiccated shell, break out from its mask, grow its wings from stubs in the sunshine, and take to its first clicking flight. By then the shadows of waterside trees had moved out across the river. I had drunk my frigerated beer and eaten my sandwiches. When the shadows were across to the other bank I went home, my rod unused, still a little mazed, as the West Country word was, in the eternity of sun and air. The female flies which had hatched and survived at noon were now wearing the

I Make a Hatchery

hues of sunset, having mated with the spinners, and were dropping their eggs upon the water.

Returning to the bridge just before dusk, I saw mist drifting down the valley. Windless air flows as water, and since sunset the colder air of the high moor had been moving down into the coombes and valleys. When it touched the bridge, its chill was upon me. The late egg-laying flies seemed to have lost heart, or life, for no more rises showed on the surface. The innumerable tongues of the water, upon stone and rock and root, were muted.

The mist spread out upon, or arose from, the meadows. Star-points, which before had been wavering in the gentle ripples of spreading trout-rings, were dimmed. How quickly the benison of the day had gone, the feelings of eternity, which is sunshine, with it. The spirit, like that of the ephemeral flies, sank down. What was a man's life, his hopes, set against the rocks, themselves but whirling atoms sprung from outer space? How did it differ, essentially, from that of fish or winged insect, except that for a brief while man's eyes beheld the stones and trees and ferns and intervolving streams, the birds of water—ousel, sandpiper, heron, kingfisher, grey wagtail, each one a morsel of happiness twisted with anxiety, each one owning or claiming for its span a vision of this pleasaunce, this valley of almost complete seclusion, which for week upon week had seemed to be my very own, wherein the spirit of wonder could spread to all life about it, until the illusion arose that such things were eternal; but when I was gone, what would remain of the self which found such wonder there?

Night was come upon the valley. Canopies of trees showed above drowning fog. I knew that it was not wise for a man to think himself beyond the bones of his being, to where Time was but empty space, in which the frailty of life was as tenuous as its spiritual purpose. I told myself that I had better go home; but at that moment the salmon locked in the shallow water half-rolled upon the surface, and looking down, I saw its glimmering form moving upstream. It was making for the shallower water which poured over the stickle into the head of the pool, where the small pied woodpecker was sleeping within its wooden bottle. There the estranged fish would lie most of the night, in colder water from the rock. What courage, what power to endure, was implanted within the salmon! So from the abyss, with frailty, but with certainty when inspiration arose, the poets had sung, the Spirit singing through them. That was the answer—to trust to life, to buoy oneself in the flow of Time, to learn to submit, and never to despair.

By the Clay Pit I watched the samlet, the first-hatched, as it hovered just off the main current of the leat and slashed at any midge or little water-fly floating down. Watercress now grew at the sides of the streamlet, and in the roots lived shrimps, daphnae and larvae of sedge and ephemeridae. There was plenty of food.

Once I saw it beside a stone, its gill-covers opening and closing faster than usual, showing a streak of red each time. Two shrimps were wedged in its mouth. It was an hour before the samlet had completely gorged the pair, wedded in death as in life.

At Last, a Dry-fly Purist!

I fished one day when the air was pressing upon the
valley. By now I had some dry flies tied on barbless
hooks, and the end of the gut cast, or leader, was a
single black horse-hair. Skill would be needed to play a
fish upon such slight tackle; and to bring it, wearied out,
to the net required two things: one, to keep a tight line,
so that the barbless hook was not shaken from the bony
sides of its jaw, two, quickness to release the strain, trust-
ing to the slightest of tensions upon the rod top, should the
fish jump clear of the water and become suddenly a heavy
weight able to snap the horse-hair.

In brogues and waders, I went through the clanging iron
gates, while horseflies flew towards me, eager for blood. I
lumbered on, protected by swallows flying around my
dressed-up form. A deadening heat filled the valley. The
sky was white and hurt the eyes. Hot blasts of air were
rising, to churn with other fiery streams and make elec-
tricity, which charged the dry air until, able to carry no
more, the invisible clouds would release their flashing
shocks into the earth.

I entered the water by the foundations of one of the
washed-out, eighteenth-century dams. It was hot. I sat on

the bank, feet in water, and unhooking my hackle fly, rubbed grease on the upper length of the gut, and upon the first dozen feet of line. My lure meanwhile was burnishing itself in the sun. The gamecock hackles glistened as I spread them to wheel-shape; and winding in line until only the glinting gut-cast was floating free, I stuck the aluminium butt-spear into turf, and lit my pipe. This done, I soaked my old sock and put it over the bottle of light ale, afterwards standing both upon a crevice of rock, in the sun.

The air was less oppressive over the water, as I waded and fished upstream. No fish rose. After half an hour, or two hundred yards, and fifty casts, I came to the dark oak trunk, noting that fresh spraints of an otter lay on the moss near its base. Had he driven all fish into hiding? Next, upon a sandy scour, I found the fresh foot-marks of a heron. A large eel wriggled up the stream beyond the roots. I threw my fly again, and went on slowly, fishing up to the Wheel Pool; but not one rise. Where were the fish? Was it too bright? Put down by atmospheric pressure? My tweed hat felt tight on my head; I had dropped it in the river by error, and either it had shrunk or my head had swelled. I chucked it on the bank, and sat down. Then I noticed swarms of tiny flies moving just over the water, at the same moment that midges began to bite my neck. Were they the same insects? I lit my short pipe again to keep them away, not wanting to use the volatile oil on my fingers, lest it affect the fly. Trout were said to have no sense of smell, but I doubted it. If eels could smell, why not trout?

Nothing in the Wheel Pool. Had someone limed the water, killing all the resident fish? I stuck my rod once more in the turf, and plunging through the stickle below the Fireplay, sat down in oak-tree shade, upon the loose gravel bank grown with docks and littered with sticks. Heat deadened the air. My absurd clothes irked me. The oil bottle, with brush set in cork pressed into a turned box-wood top, hung from the second button of my jacket. The liquid had stained both leather strap and an area of cloth in the front of the coat. It was a useless dangling nuisance; I never used it, I took off the bottle and threw it away; then went after it, and put it back in place, for the sake of the friend who had given it to me. I would present it, when I got home, to my wife; she must learn to fish, and get away from the house sometimes, and be the companion she was before the children came.

As I sat there, a corvine commotion arose in the air, and looking towards the viaduct, I saw a swirl of jackdaws about a carrion crow which was flapping heavily with a large object in its beak, which it dropped. Made curious by the sight, I walked up the river bank and crossed over by a ford, used by carts to get gravel, judging by the breaks in the banks there. Under the tall bridge lay the sock which had covered my bottle. The thought of hot beer made me hurry to the place where I had entered the river: there lay the bottle upon its side, the ale within being anything but cold. At least my package of sandwiches, cheese and watercress, had not been filched by the time I got back to the gravel bank.

I put the bottle in the shallows, where water ran over it, and waited for it to cool. Meanwhile I threw off jacket, waders, brogues, socks, shirt and vest, feeling easier.

Lolling there in the shade, I noticed a faint lipping of water across the stream, where a current, marked by a few bubbles, moved slowly under the alders at the bend. I decided that it was a small fish, and watched the water, while tobacco smoke strayed pleasantly from my pipe.

This pipe, scarcely as long as my little finger, was designed for smoking while fishing in the horsefly season. I had lost two longer pipes, knocking them out of my mouth in the early days when striking at 'keds', which infested the meadows in early summer. By now I had invented a technic for their destruction, so sure that I welcomed the low note of one's approach. Allowing it to pitch, I waited until it had lost caution, and greedily started to sink a well into my flesh with its proboscis; then, with a light and oblique stroke of the palm, it was rolled up, to fall into the river. No more wild strikings, losing pipes and composure! A light touch was enough to break the ked's frame without smear of cadaver. I became skilful in their destruction, a minor sport when wading in the river. Many a score were sent floating away, but I never saw a trout rise to the wreckage.

They were, in their way, wonderful flies, with great batteries of eye-lenses, some of which gleamed deep ruby red, others sapphire green and cobalt blue; but for all this massed searchlight effect, they found the wrong host.

As smoke arose from my pipe, I noticed another lip in the narrow stream moving slowly, its bubbles hardly rocking, under the far bank. The slightest of breaks in the surface appeared about two feet in front of the first lipping of water. It seemed a shame to throw a fly at a poor unsophisticated little parr, but I waved it idly to and fro, while still sitting down, before throwing the line across to fall lightly, with an S loop between cast and rod point for the mid-river current to take away, thus allowing a moment or two before the lure was dragged. The hackled

At Last, a Dry-fly Purist!

Poacher, well cocked up, rode down among the bubbles, an amber whirl of light. It rocked: I flicked slightly; and to my surprise, a strong fish was on. I played it cautiously, on my knees, and let it run down to the pool, lest it disturb others in the run opposite. After three minutes it came to the net, and was about half a pound, young and golden.

When my fly was dry, its hackles set again, I threw across the rapid mid-stream to my narrow movement of bubbles, noting while I did so that the myriads of tiny flies, like smuts, had apparently moved up the river from below. They drifted slowly this way and that, in clouds a few inches above the water. My fly rode down lightly among the bubbles, was sucked in, and I was playing another good fish. This, too, was led back to the pool, and when it came out, it was two ounces heavier than the first.

I seemed to have made a discovery. Kneeling in the same marks in the gravel, I got a third fish, about a yard above the place where the first had taken my fly. So that was where they fed, beyond the throat of the pool, on the other side of the main stream or current, where they could idle, and let food drift into their mouths. My tame Loch Levens waited in the pool itself, for the figure in the tree to create their 'rise'; the native fish got beyond the head of the pool, where the least effort was needed to take down-drifting flies.

In six or seven feet of that bubbled meander of water, I took eight fish, one behind the other, without disturbing those in front, since every time I hooked a fish, it dashed back to the pool, with the instinct of safety in depth. The biggest fish was in the foremost place, beside a mossy rock. It weighed, on my small spring-balance, one pound three ounces. All were brown trout, all had small mouths; and when we ate them later, the two largest had faintly pink flesh.

This at first puzzled me, for the native brown trout had flesh that was, when cooked, greyish white. The lack of colour was due to the diet of the peaty water, which was acid.

As I have mentioned, limestone or chalk streams abound with shrimps and snails; an acid stream is poor in under-water life. A four-year trout in a river near its peaty source might weigh barely three ounces; lower down, where the water had some traces of artificial fertilizers washed from fields, a fish of the same age might be six ounces. But both had white flesh. Had there been any lime-stone, instead of shillets of shale and iron, in the river-bed, the average six-ounce fish at four years might have been two pounds in weight, or over; and with pink flesh. Two of the fish I caught that sultry afternoon were pale pink inside, while their red spots were correspondingly pale in hue. Why was this?

I thought that they must have got pink flesh while feed-ing in salt water. They had been down to the sea, where their pale flesh had become incarnadined. I had seen sea-trout—the peal of the west—taken in nets in the estuary. They were obviously of two kinds, I thought: the one like a small salmon; the other like brown trout upon which liquid silver seemed to have been washed, impermanent like hot solder which splashes when it falls but does not bind. The one was a true migratory fish, akin to the salmon; the other, an accident, a casual, a stray.

These brown trout had returned from their salt-water feeding by way of the fenders I had opened with my crowbar.

At Last, a Dry-fly Purist!

That evening I marched back to the cottage with some satisfaction; and after drinking both tea-pot and kettle dry, decided to go for a swim in the pool below Humpy Bridge.

Bathing in the sea has its joys: the wide shore in summer, with no south-westerly to destroy the 'glassie, cool, translucent wave', to harry it to brutal bashings, snarling in under-tow and drag; the green rollers that slap lightly, having no weight behind their fling, whose pale walls break upon the head, and hang pearl-like tears upon the eyes. But here, in the pool, was another joy, in amber water without taste, into which one could put one's face, and float, imagining oneself to be an otter, gazing for trout; but without passion. Or one could swim down slowly, to search in dim underwater light the holes in the mossy face of the weir apron, and along the stones of the embankment walls, and see not so much as a tail vanishing. Where then were my two-score of Loch Levens? The pool was about twelve yards square. The children watching from the bridge above, and then from the banks, saw no darting of scared fish. Had they been driven downstream by otters? Had poachers dropped, by night, a weighted screw-top bottle with water and carbide inside, which had exploded and thrown out poison gas which had dissolved in the water? Or that other trick, an old stocking filled with chloride of lime? I had found a night-line in one of the stickles, baited with a mullhead; the big trout fed in shallow water at night, where a miller's thumb was said to be an irresistible bait.

Swimming the breast stroke languidly in the middle stream pouring down from under the centre arch, idly keeping my position against the mild summer flow, I saw the luminous ripple-reflections playing under the stone arch. I was bodiless; bubbles rode down level with the recording caves of my eyes. I swam as slowly as I could, without sinking. My mind felt cool and clear as the water, I was but a flow of water-feeling. Yellow mimulus flowers growing at the base of the middle stone pier—said to be a garden stray—were being sprayed by an almost invisible mist from the falls. A sun-bow shifted its fragmentary red and blue sheens as I swam aslant the stream, and floated into still water. Putting my head down again, I was surprised to see the number of sodden branches lying on the bottom. They could just be touched by my toes when I floated upright, and then sank under.

So dispassionate was the feeling of swimming into a mild current that I went back to the middle stream again, to see and feel once more the bubbles rising past my eyes and cheeks. Now the children were splashing and shouting and trying to swim in the shallows behind me, where the westering shades of the alders spread over the gravel covered by six or seven inches of rapid flow. The water of the pool was blackish-green, the bubbles were of jade. Dark water-flies, sedge and alder, now were passing in curious flight before my eyes, climax of their water life.

Swimming lazily, I saw the nose of a trout under the stone wall, where a narrow stream moved but slightly. I watched, and saw its neb again. The fish was quietly sucking in spent flies as they were borne in the fall from the eastern arch. The drove of living flies were weaving and shifting over the water, level with my eyes. While I rested, one hand on the mossy rock by the mimulus flowers, a fly lit on my wet forehead. I held up my hand, and the fly ran upon it. Its wings, pent-shaped, showed it to be of the sedge family. It had two long delicate horns, like silver wire, stretching out from its head. Slowly I put my arm under water. Silverhorns skated down beside a bubble, then arose and joined the wedding flight. I felt that these insects were happy, my relaxed body shared that happiness. I, like them, was part of the 'ceaseless flow of the fountain'.

While I floated there, after the children had run home, a family of kingfishers flew through the arches of the bridge. There were seven young ones and two parent birds. They had nested in the eroded bank of a meadow below Boundary Bridge, in a domed room at the end of a long tunnel pecked out. Here was the sun-bow broken up, made animate. The young birds were not so brightly coloured as their parents, whose backs were green as a copper flame. The two old birds cried out as they saw my head, uttering keen hard cries, or little prolonged shrieks, as they sped away downstream, to be followed, after hesitating flight around the pool, by the seven young ones. I climbed out and lay on the grass above, afterwards dressing leisurely, and strolled back to the house, feeling at peace with myself, and therefore with all the world. But seated at my writing-table once more, I found that nothing of value would come from my pen.

I did not realize it then; indeed for some years the simple fact was hidden from me—not only did I not know enough about my subject, but I had not felt enough about it, to transmute both knowledge and feeling into art.

One day, motoring from London to Devon, I stopped beside a river bridge, the air above which was white with mayflies. Looking over, I saw trout of all sizes, some of them four- and five-pounders, in the streams of water between weed-beds. The plants had white flowers, with yellow pistils, on long tresses waving in the river. The very plants I needed for my water! I kneeled upon the bank, pulled a string of water-crow's foot from its root, and saw how extraordinarily numerous were the nymphs and larvae of the *ephemeridae* crawling on the fronds. Fresh-water shrimps flipped along the stems, many with their smaller wives held in their arms. I bought two large pails from the village shop, and filled them with weed.

When I got home, I waded immediately into the river and planted lengths of *ranunculus fluvitans* under stones, spacing them in different runs and eddies. Mentioning this in The Fisherman's Arms a week or two later, I was told by a retired colonel of the Army Pay Corps that my work was a waste of time, that freshets would tear up the weed by the roots, and what plants were not deracinated would have their tender bines cut to pieces by shifting shillets. Undeterred, I fetched more pailfuls of water-buttercup and planted them out, hoping they would hold, and even spread, though the chalk-stream nymphs and eggs on the bines were likely to die in acid water.

A thunderstorm broke over the moor a week or two later, and rains followed. It was some days before the fresh fined down, and I could see the bed of the river again. Every bine, laid under its flat stone, was buried.

'What did I tell you?' said the colonel at The Fisherman's Arms one evening. 'Your weeds haven't the hope of a snowflake in hell. However, it was a good effort. One lives and learns, my boy.'

Canadian Backwoodsman

When in the middle of August an invitation came from New York to fish in Canada at the beginning of the fall, I was at once in two minds, between desire to escape from my study and reluctance to go so far away from my trout. Habits, both good and bad, are hard to break. What would happen when I was not there to look after my fish? This feeling, when subjected to thought, showed it to be but reluctance to give up habit.

I decided to go; and having fetched another hundredweight sack of fish food from Dulverton, I bought a tourist ticket from Southampton to Quebec, for mid-September. My wife and elder son said they would feed the fish daily from the bridge, and also in the Fireplay Pool. Herons, otters, poachers—the fish must take their chances.

It was my first crossing of the North Atlantic. The weather was calm, the sun shining by day, the stars by night. It was strange to hear young Canadian students, returning from vacation in Europe, speak of the Dipper, which we called the Plough. Why dipper? What was a dipper? A can, with handle, for scooping water. Canada was still a pioneering country. I looked forward to fishing in Quebec Province, where my host was a member of a Fish and Game Club, with territory of many hundreds of square miles. How would the Poacher compete, in strange lakes and rivers, with the large flies used there, with such romantic names and colours—Gold Ribbed Hare's Ear, Grizzly King, Montreal Silver and Parmachene Belle?

Across the slightly swelling wastes of the Atlantic, and far away in the grey world of water arose little columns of spray, from my first whales. Shipboard friendships among the young on holiday, in such weather upon an azure sea, were of the golden age. And the first sight of the American continent! Remote in the mist of the fishing banks was a low blue suggestion, Newfoundland of the explorers. Far away seemed the valley under the moor. The only physical link was in the thought that this was the same sea into which my stream returned its tribute, and the same spirit that had made the salmon's shape around the coasts of Britain had breathed upon these greater waters of the St. Lawrence estuary, so that salmon were in being here, to bear the spirit in thought when it felt the loneliness of travel.

Two days gliding up the St. Lawrence, in the channel marked by buoys great and small, some like red and white cottages, with flowers that were lights. No siren cries came from them, the nights and days were clear, and as we moved westward the green shores of the New World revealed their detail: cows, homesteads, rocks, birds. Then Quebec, the Château Frontenac on the heights, the board walk below, wide and far beholding, a vast esplanade reminding the traveller that Canada was a land of forests as well as of water. A night train to Montreal, arrival in early morning, waffles and maple syrup for breakfast, with eggs

Canadian Backwoodsman

fried on both sides, and coffee; a wait for the sleeper from New York to steam into the station. It had been arranged that both I and my host's son should wear each a cerise band around a sleeve, for mutual recognition. I had thought out that one band was enough, so had omitted mine.

I saw him as soon as he saw me; he also lacked a cherry-coloured armband; and after greetings we entrained for Brandon Province. Slowly, stopping at every station among the woods, we advanced upon our destination. It was wonderful to feel so leisurely, so carefree. I liked the pink and green paint on the wooden houses and sheds of the stations. At last we were there, and getting into a sedan, rode through more woods, over bumpy tracks, to the reserve of the Fish and Game Club. I had imagined a wild camp life, with shelters of balsam branches, fires and haunches of venison roasting on sapling spits; possibly log cabins; I was not prepared for this New Yorkers' luxury camp, with large wooden buildings, tablecloths and silver, a chef, comfortable bunk beds with running water basins; in fact, civilization.

But it was a good life. We ate fish with flesh a rich pink, served with hot sauce; wild turkeys with sweet potatoes and corn; blueberry pies with yellow crusted cream. And men so friendly that the novice from Elizabethan thatch and cob declined hurriedly an offer to join an after-dinner game of poker, with cigars and hard liquor, in one of the log cabins. These, he considered, were Wall Street tycoons, millionaires who played the markets and spoke of steels and coppers and names such as du Ponts, Socony, Shellenbarger, Hoover and Al Capone. Not for him and his few dollars bourbon and whiterock with ice, jackets off and sleeves rolled up under the hanging electric lights, while on the walls hung stuffed heads of moose and caribou, and enamelled fish with crimson bellies, those big ones that rolled up at Grand Dam last May, before the midges came to drive all back to the big city. Later he heard that the stakes at poker were dimes, not grands.

I had a guide, René, a Canuck, or French-Canadian. Around us were lakes and the river. There were corduroy paths through the forest by which we went on *portage*, each guide carrying his hunter's canoe reversed upon his head. The fishing places were allotted daily; we set out after breakfast, and returned for dinner before nightfall.

My small rod was pronounced by my host to be of no use, with its single dry fly; so I took the nine-feet Hardy of split Palakoma cane. The British flies were likewise no good. Soon my gut leader was equipped with local flies, three large gaudy objects which were flung away from the canoe being gently paddled around some dark tarn, and drawn back, with small jerks, through the water. This was very dull fishing, dragging flies like variations of the Stars and Stripes among the lily pads, and not caring much whether there was a strike or not. What I wanted to do was to try my gamecock hackle in the river.

Next day, while on *portage* to another tarn, accompanied by an amiable young doctor, I saw what, at home, would have been wonderful dry-fly water under a tall cascade, where the river poured down a face of rock ten feet above me. So I told René the guide to put down the canoe from off his head, and while he rested I fitted up my two-ounce rod, and advanced cautiously, bending low, to try a side-stream where bubbles rode down quietly. There, surely, a big one would roll up, to be presented with British casualness to my host, later to adorn his cabin—the fabulous four-pounder caught by the Englishman who showed the water-flag-wagglers how to bring 'em out. When after a few casts no fish rose, the doctor, who was keen as I was, climbed up the rock and standing above, clear-cut against the sky, let down his line and leader and trio of flies to dangle in the stream before me, possibly, I thought, to hook the imminent roller-up before my fly did its deadly work.

'Five dollars—who gets the first one—how about it?'

He was an amiable fellow, and I did not like to say that his moving outline was likely to put any fish down, as he flicked his large and gaudy lures beside my little hackled fly. Honours were even—we whipped water in vain.

The river was low, the summer had been exceptionally dry, its rocky course was bare, save for the dark-brown flow in its centre, and the wide lagoons or lakes through which it meandered. The guide sat on the gunwale of the canoe, behind me and my rod. There were four canoes, one for each member of the party. None of us had yet caught a fish. We were driving forward through a long stretch almost stagnant between swamp and scrub when I felt a sudden loud blast behind me. It wrinkled the water by my canoe as pellets whizzed away to scratch the surface a hundred yards ahead. One of our party, who had brought guns that morning as well as rods, was practising.

Soon I saw the need for this. The canoes having been beached, we went hunting. The Doc carried a shot-gun-cum-rifle; my host, a repeater twelve-bore. I, a gunless guest, was put in the place of honour, to lead through the scrub. Suddenly another blast passed my left ear. In front on the path were piping cries of alarm, a flurry of soft wings. A crumpled leaf-hued hen lay six feet away. The Doc, who read *The Saturday Evening Post* at night, said with a small boy's enthusiasm, 'I guess I've gotten my first wild turkey!'

'Well done,' I said, edging my way to the rear of the column. Polite phrases followed. The Doc offered me his gun. I explained that I had given up shooting, but would find it interesting to watch things from the rear. My host, who was also my American publisher, explained to the ever-hospitable Doc that I was a nature lover, like Thoreau.

'I get it! That pond at Walden!' I was allowed to trail along behind.

It was not wise to go off by oneself in the woods. Other hunters were likely to mistake movement for buck, moose, turkey or even skunk. But apart from that, I could not feel Thoreau-like in that country. I learned that I was not the only one. There was sadness in my guide's face. Soft-voiced René spoke of the ice that was coming, of long frozen days and white nights of near-Arctic winter, of deep snows lying over a bare land whence whole forests had been lost in the tremendous fires which had, the year before, returned hundreds of square miles of vegetation and soil to ash and grey rock again. I found the absence of small bird-life sad, while the everlasting quiet sunshine seemed to be brooding upon its own defeat. Struggle was eternal between the elements, but they had been the outward means of fashioning, out of tensions, what had been wantonly lost.

I began to feel the need for my home. I lay about in my cabin, unable to read, feeling it impossible to write. Nearly all my mind was in Devon. How were the boys faring? And my tame trout? My thoughts, like those of the birds which had already gone, went as with wings on migration —home, home to the candle-lit casement windows in the valley.

And then the first mail arrived from England, some of it bearing a postmark with the power to make the heart start almost with anguish. All was well; the apples were picked, the pears not yet ripe; Baby Margaret was a darling, the two little boys were so good and helpful. Daily they accompanied their mother to the bridge, to 'feed Daddy's fishes'. The trout were still there, both above and below the bridge. The weather was simply splendid, no rain, but sun day after day. It was hoped that I was having a splendid time, I was to be happy, and not to worry about anything at home.

The springs of my being flowed again, and I set out happily on *portage* next morning, to learn on my return that someone had been catching fish by trolling in one of the very deep lakes; three splendid specimens of *fontinalis* lay on a dish on the table in the club house, native brook trout with marbled green backs and vermilion bellies—the male in spawning dress. Warmed by roaring fires of split birchwood on the hearth, we ate them for dinner after the labours of the day. I still had a vision of catching two- and three-pounders on my hackle fly which, I had already boasted, was the most deadly fly in England.

Blueberry pickers poached the club waters. They fished with worms in the stickles, or jabbles as they were called, leaving their nut-wands on the bank afterwards. There were game wardens, but too many berry pickers. They lived wild off land and water. I refused to fish with a worm. It was dry fly, or nothing.

The best place in the club preserve, I decided, was Grand Dam. This was a structure of spruce poles built across the river, for the purpose of holding back water. Above the dam was an artificial lake of some hundreds of acres. The original idea had been to cut the spruce and cedar forests around the lake, haul the boles or logs to the shore, tip them in and get them behind the dam; then the floods of autumn, and rush of lake water when the dam was dynamited, would bear them down to the mills. But fire had arrived before the felling, and the dam remained.

There was a wooden bridge or platform across the narrow end of the dam, and here was a favourite place for anglers to stand, casting down their lures, hoping to get the enormous trout ranged below, head to the underwater streams issuing from the foot of the dam. The fish took no notice of the artificial mice wiggled on the surface six feet above them; or of the wooden plugs painted with all sorts of colours and every kind of eye, fin, tail, spot, bar and hung with sets of treble hooks on swivels; nor of artificial frogs, worms, eels, grasshoppers, minnows, wasps, bees and other bugs. Why did they not take? Were they feeding on something washed under the bottom of the dam? If so, why did not one of the fish sometimes dash away, show a flash as it turned to take its food, and then return to its place?

'They might be bar-flies in an East-side flop-house, for all the interest they take in what is going on, I guess. Say, what d'you think they're there for, Henry?'

'I've no idea, Doc.'

Doc then proceeded to tie a new leader to his line. He had, he guessed, the answer. Lovingly he showed me his last-ditch fly, which was, he whispered, unobtainable commercially. It was a secret fly, invented by Mr. DuBois; he had managed to get one. He winked solemnly at me. The deadly fly had a down-to-earth name, Never-Was. It had an orange wing, tied with backward slant, a green hackle, and four whisks or tails of what looked to be dark green water-moss.

'First I guess I'll try my Inch Worm,' said the Doc, lovingly.

Inch Worm had a pale green silk body, with hackles of the same colour. He had a hunch, too, that a Fan Wing Pink Lady might start off a Bull Market. He spoke the name softly to himself—Fan Wing Pink Lady. His eye glowed. I caught his enthusiasm, his affection. We became buddies.

'Sounds like a killer, Doc.'

'I guess you're right, Henry.'

Down went the Fan Wing Pink Lady to stroke the water. After twenty minutes of vain luring, he said, 'I guess this beats me, Henry. I reckon that they're all bucks down there, too.'

Feeling very much a backwoodsman in my new white tight-fitting corduroy trousers, seal-skin belt, knee-high mocassins and red flannel shirt, I said, 'I guess the Fan Wing Pink Lady don't appeal to them, Doc.'

'I guess that's so, Henry. Wale, I guess I'll try Never-Was.'

This fly justified both name and performance. 'Wale, I guess I'll be going back for a little something. Don't you want to come with me, and have one?'

'I'll be along presently, Doc.' I now felt the piscatorial fire descend upon me. I must get one of those monster red-bellies. I tried to think.

Above the dam the lake water was deep. Standing there, I wondered why lean fish were suddenly rising, or rather swirling up in boils, and going down again, not showing themselves. What were they taking, a foot beneath the surface? I could see nothing there. However, a rise was a rise, and should be fished. I had my Hardy rod, and in my box a moth-eaten Coachman, its white wings frayed away to the stub. It looked like nothing when I had cut away its brown hackle and pared its peacock herl body. The boiling rises continued, about one every half-minute. Could the fish be playing? And why were they so lean?

A gentle breeze was blowing from the bank, out across the water, not enough to ruffle the surface: a gossamer waft of air. This was useful when I began to throw out my line, with slower and slower sweepings back and fore, until about eighteen yards of tapered enamelled silk were out. Then pulling a loop lest the final throw whip back, I cast my fly. It fell straight, with an imperceptible flip into the water; I worked it back, as though the shrimp were swimming zigzag; and immediately a fish had taken it.

The plug, mouse, frog, wasp, bee and other bug men stroking water below the dam stopped to watch. The Englishman had caught a fish. It came, after a strong fight, to the net: a two-pound brook trout. I cast again, another was on. René my guide was flushed, not so much with tuberculosis, poor fellow (many French-Canadians suffered from this, confined in cabins all the winter, living on their club wages and tips) but that his hunter was doing what the others could not do. I knew I had no special skill; but I did not know, until later, that the long, lithe fish I was taking, one after another, were hen fish; nor realize that the big fish below the dam were cocks, waiting there to get to the hens above the dam. Perhaps they were drawn by scent, if fish can smell. I was to feel sure, in the light of later knowledge, that they were waiting there to get to the spawning beds. The hens 'boiling up' above the dam were all females that I took that afternoon, to return with a dozen two-pounders to the club house, all killed on the moth-eaten and pared but otherwise dry-fly Coachman. The expected look of congratulation in my host's face was absent. And no wonder—the limit for each rod per day was two brace of fish.

However, my lapse was soon forgotten in the great event of the fall season, which occurred the next day. A bull moose, rarest quarry to be seen in all the club territory—so rare in Canada, indeed, that each hunter was permitted by law to shoot but one in his lifetime—fell to my host's rifle. That night, and for every night following, we had moose steaks at dinner. They were the most tender meat I ever tasted, being almost as soft as pounded spinach. They had a suggestion of the flavour of grouse, perhaps from a diet of heather and blueberries. Dear old John Macrae was greatly pleased: a lifelong ambition had been gained.

During our last week we went on *portage*, father, son and guest, to a lake which we fished for two days, sleeping at night in a log cabin on an islet. Enormous fire on hearth of rough grey stones, bunk beds in cabins smaller than those on liners for tourist passengers, oil lamps on the pinewood panelled walls. I found it suited me more than the luxurious cabins, with ordinary beds, on the shore of the lake by which stood the club house. We three bathed naked in the early morning light, when mist lay on the water; and echoing through the mist, with silver startling loveliness, came the cry of the loon fishing half a mile away in the centre of the lake. My friend fetched his express rifle, and sent a bullet flipping across the surface, with little splashes, in the direction of the bird, a great northern diver; not to shoot it, but in greeting. The bird gave a cry of wild beauty, like bubbles being broken, a cry with the quality of precious metal as it rose and flew away over the forest, to another lake, perhaps, where man was not.

René cooked fish which John caught on a present from the departed Doc, the Never-Was. At midday our guide made a fire, over smooth stones from the shore of the lake, and laid the fish on the embers. We ate pieces in our fingers, while René carved me a drinking cup from a burr cut off a golden birch tree. All the hunters of the club had these cups, which they carried by means of raw moose-hide strung on a button of their hunting shirts. The cups were dipped in the streams when one was thirsty. I now felt to be one of them, in my red hunting shirt and moccasins with hide laces to the knee. I had bought myself, too, a mackinaw coat, of purple and red chequers, the next best thing to a bullet-proof vest, I realized later, when I saw the published figures of deer and hunters shot in the woods of New York State during that year. Both were in the thousands. More hunters were shot than deer. New York State, I hasten to add, was not Canada, where in the various clubs a higher standard of gunmanship prevailed.

Some wild life remained in what was left of the woods after the forest fires. Chipmunks came to take orange peel as we sat at lunch—small squirrels with badger markings of black and white, and tails held cockily upwards. The maple trees were turning deep, deep red; the fall silence was upon the forest primeval; stars flashing at night; the air was still, the brown leagues of lake water unruffled; René's gentle face resigned to the coming of the ice. When the time came to leave, I had to admit to my friend that the American method of fishing was superior to my own. I never rose a fish to the red-hackle.

The rest of my adventures in the New World, which extended from the fall to the spring of the New Year, when my wife came to fetch me home, are outside the scope of this little book. I brought back with me, among other souvenirs, the drinking cup carved by René from the gall of a golden birch. It was carved in the shape of an otter, done in authentic flowing lines with considerable skill; and it hangs from one of the beams of Canadian pine in my Devon studio as I write of that faraway time.

I Stare at Water and Make Dams

The first thing I did upon my return to Devon was to go to the river. My elder son had taken on the job of feeding the fish, accompanied by his nurse, during his parents' absence. There my trout were, ready to dash up and seize particles of floating food, showing at the turn blue-white gleams of the spring sky. I walked up the river bank, looking for all the familiar things—the otter's ant-hill, where he left his spraints; sites of proposed dams; weeds planted in the quieter stretches. Winter floods had run off their field and plantation washings, the water was strong but clear; grey, brown, pink, blue and white stones were visible on the river-bed in sunlight . . . and yes! waving short tassels of crow's-foot. The pay colonel in The Fisherman's Arms was wrong; the weeds had held.

It was cold weather, with wind from the north-east; but the light was coming back. I saw a salmon lying at the tail of the pool below Humpy Bridge, a thin dark object, with a suggestion of gleam upon its shadowy lankness. Was this a kelt which had spawned, and 'mended' itself? I had read of fish, thin and wasted after spawning, recovering to assume the silver of smolt-hood when dropping back

I Stare at Water and Make Dams

to the sea where, in the biblical simplicity of the language of netsmen, they would 'clean themselves'.

I forgot about the kelt when I went to feed the Loch Levens the next morning, until I saw the long gleam of a fish turning under water, a trout gripped across its back and held, to be taken slowly down to the invisible bottom of the pool. Did the kelt gorge the pounder, head first? I did not know, nor did I see it again, when I fed a week later.

As the sun made the days wider my delight grew with the clumps of green tassels beginning to put out long bines, which waved above the planted places. As they grew longer, I waded in the water to examine them. Freshets had buried the original clumps; into those accumulations of stream-lined sandy silt the white roots crept, making multiple holdings, and from each root new green tassels had grown. Every time a freshet came down, more silt was left among the stems, which made more roots, which in turn sprouted more shoots. They grew longer, and in late spring white flowers of crow's-foot, each with its yellow stamens, were lying dreamily upon the surface.

I was beginning now to see water in terms of factual knowledge, for a book on a salmon's life I hoped to write one day. Looking down one morning from the road bridge, where my beat ended, I saw that the flow in a river was made up of several streams, moving at varying speeds and in different directions. Some streams were running; others were being pushed aside; in places the water was hardly in movement. This was in part the effect of the irregular bed. Gazing down in a cool shade, entranced by the crystal clearness of the water, I made out stones of all sizes, the larger of brown rock grown with moss, the smaller ones worn smooth and protruding through the gravel. Shafts of sunlight piercing the leaves of the tree growing below the bridge on the right bank revealed the many hues of the stones—black, pale pink, white as of marble, dove-grey, blue, tawny, pale yellow. Beyond this area of coloured stones, pushed there by a recent spate— one by one, gradually, each stone resisting the water—I could see the old settled bed of the river, brown. Each flake and boulder there was covered with life: little houses of sand and gravel speck, assembled and mortar'd, some in movement as their owners fed upon the brown algae, minute vegetable growths which were slippery to the hand when one lifted a stone. This was the food of small forms of life called diatoms and plankton, and of nymphs and crawlers which fed the trout in the river.

The tree just below the bridge on the right bank was a sycamore. Leaving the road, and kneeling on the bank below the tree, where the tail of the pool ran shallow and fast, I saw upon a stone, the top of which was just above the water, a multi-legged brown insect, with antennae or whiskers. It moved slowly; then it stopped, as though weary. It was a creeper of the March Brown which, I had heard, took the place of the mayfly in a stony stream lacking lime.

The creeper had lived for a year in watery darkness; now its time was come to change its world into that of air and light. Its motor, that gave it movement, was seizing. The creeper was becoming transfixed upon the stone. Its brown sheath was becoming a mask, immobilizing its entire body. Within the pellicle an intense form of change into winged life was taking place.

A caterpillar pupates, to become moth or butterfly after a prolonged period, sometimes six months; but water is more urgent than earth and air, more primeval, and everything about the world of a river seemed to be accelerated, perhaps because of its earlier association with evolved life.

The creeper was arising to become part of the air. Now it was heaving within its clawed chassis; its neck behind the bulged head was splitting; and a creature with creased stub-wings was crawling forth, to dry its wings while it trembled slightly there. If touched it would run in panic back to the water and slide away on the water-skin, racing with its legs, suggesting an inverted canoe, with outriggers and paddles, of dark, glistening brown.

The *imago* of the March Brown had left the water, a place of dreaded enemies, but of known security, for the glaring emptiness of light. Or was it dazzled, in a state of immense excitement, that air was heaven?

Left to itself, it would have dried off and then flown to hide among twigs and leaves of alders, to await twilight for the climax of its life in the dance of love—the pure sensation of instinct which men lose after they begin to think about what they feel. For the March Brown there was the love-play over the water, the delirium of mating, the fall apart from the climax of all-feeling, dropping away in the fulfilment of life, which is personal death, so that the species shall live on. For the male, emptiness and dissolution; for the female, glory of self-forgetfulness as she drops her eggs from her whisks, or ovi-positors, and then the peace that passes into night.

In a mood of unadjusted self, against my clearer knowledge, I touched the new-risen March Brown, the Great Stone Fly, the *imago* resting on the smooth islet of igneous rock: away it went skittering upon the flow of water rippling with many pressures from its stony bed. As I watched there was the least break in the surface, a view of brown blue-nostrilled neb, a slight extra sucking noise among the stone-and-water cries of the river. The life within the March Brown was gone into another form of life.

Its pellicle lay upon the stone, brittle and empty. As I was picking it up my elder son's face appeared among the ivy upon the parapet of the bridge.

'That was my fly, I was watching it!'

Climbing up to the lane above, I showed the discarded water-uniform of the fly, and was about to describe its use, when he burst out, 'You put that back! That poor fly may want its coat one day!'

Staring down from the parapet of the bridge, when the child had gone away, I saw that the many streams which made up the river varied in speed, direction, depth and width. Some flowed backwards, in the eddies; others curled over like query marks, so that a trout waiting behind such a stone was seen to be facing down-river, as it watched for food in the comb of the water pouring down in front of its eyes. A trout, to breathe, must face the stream, for it breathes by opening its mouth for the water to pass through its gills, which are the equivalent of lungs, by which it takes oxygen from the water. The currents, eddies, queries, combings, jabbles, bickerings and flumes which made up the river and in which the trout had their stances were also the food-streams. When a trout balanced in its pocket of water saw a shrimp or a nymph swirling down upon a ribbon of water it darted forward, seized it, and slipped back to its place, its swim-bladders automatically adjusted through varying pressures of moving water.

I Stare at Water and Make Dams

As the springtime days went by, I learned that every trout's place in the river belonged to it by right of force. Any other trout of the same, or smaller size approaching that place was driven away. Each fish, too, had its home, or place of retreat, often in a hole under the bank, or below a stone.

Leaning over the mossy parapet of the road bridge, I experienced, with the rising buoyancy of air, a sudden elation that I was back again in the valley. Were human moods from the air? Fish certainly were affected. When the atmosphere was heavy or muggy the fish were down; they too felt heavy, being immediately susceptible to pressure upon the water, it seemed. But when the white clouds billowed into the blue halls of the wind, following Atlantic rains, how beautiful was the river in the valley, how great was my fortune to be able to live freely, my own master, beside this moorland stream which ran through quiet meadows, with oaks and beeches beside its course, and lichened alders along the banks! It was also, in hard days of the cold north-west wind, a comfort to realize that I was not alone in feelings of bleakness. The fish were as susceptible to the elements as oneself. But man was more fortunate than a fish or bird, for he could, by devotion, become an artist, to create for other men a sense of beauty that their less unconfined living sometimes denied them.

Now that the sunlight came racing with cumulus shadows over the grass, I felt the free spirit of all life arising with the air. The river surface gleamed with sky, the birds sang and played; the rooks and daws sported and tumbled in the upper air, buzzards soared in tiers, not for food, but joy; the nymphs of the olive dun broke through the silvery skin of the water, appearing as small globes of yellow-green light, to find grace. Man, as artist, must not only feel, but think. The trout came from under stones and hovers by the bank, and took up their positions in the water flow. Each position or stance or waiting place was chosen for its view of food washing past, and also that there the least energy was required to hold the body balanced in the water.

The law of profit was the law of life; no animal could work for nothing, or it would lose its life; and the energy supplied by one swimming nymph or hatched fly must not be gained with a greater expense of energy than the food replaces. So each fish had its position, where it awaited the food in its own particular stream.

The fall of the valley bottom being gradual (in comparison with mountain torrents) the bed of the river remained much the same from year to year. I was beginning to know the pools, scours, hovers, eddies; the bankside trees of oak, alder, ash, thorn, sycamore and hazel were becoming familiar marks in my life. And all the wild life about the place I felt to be my own.

I had learned where certain birds and their nests were to be found; where fish lay, the strongest fish in the best places; where the otter touched and dropped its spraints—small dark scriddicks often holding small eel- and other fish-bones—which looked like black-green lichens and most curiously smelled sweet, with a scent not unlike violets; where the heron waited to take the running sea-trout in autumn, when the leaves were changing colour beside the Peal Stone falls, where fish after fish leapt, a few inches away from the bank, and were snicked in the sharp mandibles, so frequently, that the grey bird grew tired of swallowing them, and picked out the eggs and milt of hen and cock fish respectively, leaving the limp bodies on the bank. Man was not the only destroyer; in truth, he, the earth-worm and the bee were three of the main conservators of terrestrial life.

The river was my friend, and at times my tyrannous master: or, to put it another way, I put upon it my own tyrannous image of would-be perfection. I liked my friend well, after the turn of the year—I liked it best when after winter freshets, with springs gushing full fast, the water began to flow clear again with that blue-grey volume through which its pride and joy, its child of genius, the salmon, came up from the sea. How could I re-create all this beauty in words?

I found a colony of rare birds one day, beside the river. Walking on the path through the wood below my beat, I saw three small round holes in three alders, all within five yards of one another. The holes were the size of shillings, smaller by half than the lesser spotted woodpecker's above Humpy Bridge. I recognized them at once from one I had found in Kent when I was eleven years old: they were the holes of the rare willow tit, pecked out of dead soft wood. Within, I knew without breaking open, or touching, were woven flat nests of moss, feather, willow floss and cow-hair; almost flat pads. I kept the discovery to myself, knowing that collectors would be after them if word got around.

I had come no nearer to solving the mystery of the lesser spotted woodpecker's drumming. At The Fisherman's Arms there were two theories: one, held by the Pay Corps colonel, that the bird used a dead branch as sounding-box for its glottal vibration; the other, by the judge, that the bird used its beak as a drum-stick.

I Stare at Water and Make Dams

Dippers were resident in the valley. Every half-mile or
so, there was a pair of those pied wrens of the river. The
sturdy black and white little birds walked underwater on
the gravel by holding to stones as they sought food.
Perched on a mossy rock, the cocks sang with the very
accents of the streams trickling and splashing over rock and
gravel throughout the summer days, chip of stone and
splink of water. A pair nested under an arch of Humpy
Bridge, unseen and unknown to me until, wading there
one day, I found a hanging beard of water-moss and touching it, was startled as five leaden-hued fledgelings dropped
out, one after another and swam away under water. I was
worried lest they be drowned, and damned myself for my
stupidity as the flow took them over into the deep pool,
where I could not see them. They had never flown, or left
the nest before; surely they would be drowned?

My self-reproach was due to ignorance, for all survived,
having swum under water, using their wings, from which
the quills were still not fully sprouted, as arms. They came
to the surface beside the eastern stone wall which bonded
the bank there. I saw them clinging to the water-moss on
the stones, after some minutes of searching. Their polls
were spruce and apparently unwetted, perhaps from natural
grease upon the feathers.

I left them there, to await their parents, and concealed
myself behind the parapet of the bridge. They seemed to be
at home in the river; and re-living the scene as I had
touched the nest, I recalled the momentary impression of
body-shapes in miniature resembling the Great Northern
Diver, or loon, as one had followed another out of the
nest, five in all leaving within the space of two or three
seconds. To me the shape of the young had looked much

more like diving birds than their parents. Could it be that
the species was returning from water to land as, in reverse,
otters were land beasts which comparatively recently had
turned to water for their food? While I speculated about
this, there was a pebble-chatter below me, and peering
over, I saw the parents at the tail of the pool, calling
their young to be fed.

There was another dipper's nest under the Peal Stone
Falls. The birds flew through the white curtain of dropping
water taking moss with which to make the nest, and dry
brown beech leaves with which to line it—hundreds of
flights through white water. Behind the curtain the young
were hatched, to come out later and take to water almost
naturally—in contrast to young otters, which have to be
dropped by their parents into water, because they do not
take to it naturally.

During the winter of that year I set about a job I had long
meditated, of making dams of concrete across suitable
places in the river, to raise the river level behind the
barriers, and provide better holding for fish. Cement was
ground limestone; snails would get lime for their shells, so
would shrimps. Later on, I hoped to get permission for a
more grand scheme to double or even treble the average
weight of fish. That was to order trucks of limestone,
drawn by an engine which would halt upon the viaduct;
whereupon gangs of men, fifty or so from the unemployed
in the district, would throw down the stuff, which later I
could bring to the riverside in my motor trailer. A hundred
tons would do for a start; I didn't want to strain the Great
Western Railway's viaduct. Meanwhile, the dams could
be made by mixing gravel from the waterside heaps, at the

I Stare at Water and Make Dams

ratio of one shovelful of cement for three of gravel. I bought three score potato sacks for the formes; and aided by a friend most willing to help, mixed the first batch.

Having seen how the dams above the waterfall had fared —and how the once-deep pool behind the weir of the fall had been silted with gravel, making the water there probably more shallow than it had been originally—it seemed that the dams must be made at lesser bends, which was convenient, because there the gravel beds were heaped beside the water.

It was hard work. My Clay Pit digging of two years before had merely taught the mind that there was a slower rhythm of living yet to be acquired with body work: a balance between body and brain, so that the mind, or consciousness, did not harass the body, and so cloud the contentment of being alive. That digging, however, had not been prolonged sufficiently to teach the mind that truth, once and for all—the old truth of *mens sana in corpore sano*. My body was soft above my legs, which were used to walking; and as one's mind raced before the slowness of labour, so one tended to force the work. The old hare and tortoise story. Soon the body ached; the skin of hands was dissolved; cracks appeared; gravel in shoes irked, but since leather was sodden, as also were trousers and socks, I was reluctant to stop and 'effect' a clearance. Anyway, they would be gritty again at once. Also, it was too cold to stop work. It was freezing.

At last several petrified jute sacks, each about five feet long, lay in fixed bulgings upon the gravel. The frost was not severe enough to crack the concrete. When hardened, the sacks were hauled and levered into position. The current ran fast at the bends, where the stream was corres-

I Stare at Water and Make Dams

pondingly narrow; the line of rugged concrete raised the level above, and caused turbulence with bubbled gushings below. What would happen in a flood? Would gravel be left in the channel above, making it shallow; and cause water to spread over the gravel beds beside its old course, to shift these gradually downstream?

It was too cold to stop and think. We made four dams altogether, mixing about twelve tons of batch. While this was being done, the very idea of writing was avoided as something most distasteful. The act of working in cold water was now a habit, it was stimulating, hardening, a pleasant thing with its perpetual, impersonal energy, clear as crystal as it twired past drowned shoe and knee-bone. Bending was no longer painful, the upper body was sprung from the thighs, and lean; the eyes clear, the arms tough. This was no Passchendaele winter; half a mile away was a room with a fire and dry clothes. Heigh ho unto the green holly!

By the return of spring, the woven jute of the sacks was peeling off. I found shrimps harbouring there. The pattern formed upon the concrete endured, algae grew upon the patterns, snails and limpets gathered there, taking lime to make their shells. Also nymphs crawled upon the slippery surface, grazing on the pastures of algae. I was content; but reluctant to return to my desk. Would my hand, which had also held a seven-pound axe to cut and clear the riverside scrub above the viaduct (and no murmur from Mr. Aidge-boar!) ever hold pen again, without shaking and dropping the slender vulcanite thing?

Water Play

*T*he *Fishing Gazette* was delivered regularly with other papers and periodicals by a boy on a bicycle from the local shop, which combined the retail trades of haberdasher, coal, artificial manure, lamp-oil merchants and grocer. The stock of this hamlet emporium included what was called dried tea fish, lengths of which hung for weeks in the window, salted, pale yellow, and almost as hard as wood. These were salted cod from the Newfoundland Banks. Among the slabs hung rugs, hand-brooms, carpet-beaters, hob-nailed boots, lamp wicks, printed cotton frocks and fireworks. Behind the display could be discerned the grill of a post-office desk.

In *The Fishing Gazette* I read a review of a book describing the improvements possible in rapid streams. I bought this, and was soon deep in an account of making dams of posts driven into the gravel of a river-bed, to which wire netting was fastened. The next morning I bought some larch posts from the sawmills and rolls of galvanized net from the ironmonger; and together with iron bar, wooden beetle made from a heavy round section of apple wood fitted to an ash handle, staples and hammer, hurried to the riverside.

Water Play

The idea was to fix the net to the posts, leaving a skirt which, bent at right angles to the posts, was laid upstream and held in place by gravel.

This was easier done than had been imagined. After the first day's work the body was in tune with its labours. When the first dam had been completed, a hundred yards above the Peal Stone Falls, I stood back, wet and happy, to watch leaves and other floating vegetation choking the holes in the netting. The water rose above the leaf weir; it wimpled below. But would the wire net hold in a freshet?

According to the author of the book, water pouring over the weir would churn the gravel below, making a pit into which the wire would bulge with its weight of gravel, gradually sliding forward to fill the pit. Either the gravel I had shovelled on the skirt behind was not enough, or the pit cut by water was too deep in front; for after another freshet the whole thing became horizontal, before going down to the sea, leaving two leaning posts upon which herons perched, the better to snick out fingerlings in that normally placid length of river.

Somewhat to my surprise, the potato sacks had held across the deep, fast places, where I had expected them to be shifted downstream. Some slabs had slid forward a little, but they deepened the runs and created turbulence, which was to the good.

Where the dams had been made across slight curves, I saw how the water had behaved in a manner opposite to its tenant's intentions. One had imagined that the rows of concrete sacks, where laid across wide, therefore shallow, parts of the river, would turn the shallows into pools. Actually they had made the shallows even more shallow. For a shallow existed where the flow was evenly dispread over the river-bed; and when the concrete obstacles had been heaved and levered in place, the water rose to the level of the top or sill of the new dam. The current moved on the surface at the old rate of flow; but over the river-bed it was slower. This meant that more silt was deposited than before; and when the water dropped in spring, sand, gravel and stones were piled almost to the top of the dam.

Below the dam, the turbulence of falling water had cut a series of pits. In the course of later freshets the slabs, having as it were dug their own graves, gradually slid forward and were soon covered with gravel. They were no good. Where I wanted the water deepened, the river took my obstacle out to sea. Elsewhere it interred them. As for the swift narrow streams connecting pools, where the water already foamed and sang, and where they were not really needed, the sacks of concrete held.

Walking on the bank one noon in bright sunlight, I saw an alder branch lying in a rocky stretch below the third ruinous water-slide made in the eighteenth century. There was a bine of crow's-foot entangled in the branch, which was about the size of a pea-stick. I had cut it with a hook in the early spring, but no freshet had since come down to wash it away. There it lay, lodged against a sharp tooth of rock.

I intended to fish for trout that evening, so I walked into the water to pull out the obstacle. As I balanced on a razor-edge and lifted up the branch I saw, to my surprise, lying in about a foot of crystal-clear water, a clean-run grilse of about five pounds. I stood still, slowly lowering the branch, while the drops dripped upon the rock at my feet.

As I stood there, statuesque, I wondered if this was the

Water Play

grilse I had seen a week previously from Humpy Bridge. One morning it was in the pool, lying on the gravel. I imagined that it had moved up from the estuary at night, for it was clean-run. There was normally a run of 'maiden fish' in the late spring. This was the net-fishermen's term for grilse, and who knows that it had not been handed down during the centuries? This maiden fish at my feet was silvery and shapely, with flanks not yet fallen in, the curd still being between skin and flesh. Was it the same fish that had lain on the gravel until the sun moved over the limes just inside the deer park and lit the gravel? Then it had moved into hiding under the alder roots, to come forth again at evening, and join the trout in the main stream of water cooling with the coming of night. There it had remained a while, before roving round the little area of water and taking position for the night in the jabble at the bend. The previous evening the small shapely fish was not there. Was she now below me, in about a foot of water, beside the ledge of rock upon which I stood, not daring to move?

The weed-hung branch had been the grilse's only shelter. Was she afraid to move? Could she see me? Or had the sudden blaze of the sun upon her right eye temporarily blinded her?

As quietly as possible I crept away with the branch, and put it in the water below the bank, not wanting the nymphs crawling on the water-buttercup bines to die. Having removed shoes and socks, I opened my Rolleiflex camera and crept back into the water. The sun was right for me; the fish's eye was still glazed with light, no warning shadow lessened the shine. I took four photographs, the camera lens being held about a yard above the fish. I longed for a portrait attachment, so that I could have got down to the water surface to within nine inches of the slightly spotted back, which was slightly curved. As the water moved invisibly, delicate gold lines of ripple-shadows passed over the fish, and across the sandy bottom on which she rested. Sometimes the golden reams faintly blurred the outline.

When I had taken six photographs, all I had on my roll, I bent down and stared at the grilse. Her mouth hardly opened as she took in water every three seconds. It seemed that she was asleep, for had she been afraid, or tense, she would have been breathing faster. I slid my hand along the slender 'wrist' by the tail, half-meaning to see if I could tail her. But I did not want to. Then a shock passed up my arm and the water dully drummed and a bow-wave was arrowing downstream.

That evening, before I walked up the river to fish for trout, I thought I would throw my fly, just to see what would happen, in the run above Humpy Bridge. If I caught one of the Loch Levens, I could always put it back, I told myself, as I moved into position to throw lightly my imitation of a red spinner tied to its barbless hook. Before leaving the cottage lawn, I had tied my assembly of steel, silk, tinsel and twisted gamecock hackle to a single black horse-hair, taken from a rubbing-post in the deer park.

It was a calm, mellow evening, which checked any impulse to hurry. Rises were visible in the slightly rocking water in front of me, where I stood on the gravel at the river's edge. I was about to make my first throw, standing in water to my ankles, when the maiden fish swam slowly

Water Play

up from behind me, and paused within a few inches of my feet.

Gradually I turned my head to watch her. After a while she turned on her side, in that shallow water, exposing all her flank and sinuating on the gravel, as though trying to scrape away the itch in her gill, where, I suspected, fresh-water maggots were beginning to cluster. Were they larvae of beetles, or the Fisherman's Curse soon to be adrift low over the water in clouds of winged smut as though wafted by airs too faint for one to feel—the airs made by the fanning of a myriad wings?

To rid itself of parasites, whatever they were, the fish was now pushing itself against the welt of my canvas brogue. Then she moved almost imperceptibly into deeper water, though still not deep enough to cover her back fin, and began a series of gentle rolling movements, porpoise-like. Suddenly she swam up the run, pushing waves from bank to bank; and I knew by my own calm feeling that she had not driven forward out of fear. Was she playing, in relief from the glare of day? The gold-dusty light of the sun was now gone down behind the hills. A seed-pearl shone in the sky as dark blue as the interior of a mussel-shell. This was the planet Venus, symbolizing love, and the coming of night. Night was the salmon's friend; its near presence had released an impulse of joy. Or was it but an intolerable itch, itch, itch on those gill-rakers, driving the fish to make a slashing turn in water shallower than her depth, to hurtle down the run again, making that under-water thruddling sound as she passed? Re-entering deeper water above the bridge piers, she leapt and smacked down on her side. Then up she came again, lifting herself out of water, and so to her moorings, as it were, to idle in the run, where she held her place with the slightest of sinuating movements.

While I stood there, a bine of crow's-foot drifted down. Was this a fragment of the piece that had lodged in the alder branch? As it passed, the fish seized and held it in her mouth, and then blew it out. It seemed to me to be a playful act.

The bine drifted down, one white flower riding on the surface. The grilse turned round and seized it again. Surely she was playing with the weed? I stood there until dark, filled with a calm happiness, watching the fish playing by herself—a fish confined to a few square yards of water, to a life of many perils now that she had abdicated the sea— princess among fish which had lost her kingdom—one to whom, by my stillness, I could pay tribute only in thought.

Venus shone softly in the west.

Night was come, night full of glowing suns and fluorescent lights which the salmon might see, and to which I was blind; the rocks glowing dark red, or maybe deep blue, a brown hen's feather floating down seen as purest white: the cold water flowing, flowing from the rock of the moor, ancient matter of the stars, to which the spirit of the fish was linked, in both life and death.

Death would surely come to the maiden: by disease, by gaff of poacher, by teeth of otter, by packs of hunting eels, unless the rains came. I longed for a freshet, but the weather, day after day, remained calm and sunny.

The sun shone and shone; could this be an English summer? The last fresh was in April, and then the river was far from being bank-high. That rush of coloured water was

Water Play

not even strong enough to dislodge the heaps of brambles and willow branches which I had cut and thrown into the stream during March. There they lay, dry and bleached, the moorhen's old nest two feet above the water-level. The willow branches had put out roots, many inches long, into the mass of rotten leaves and wood accumulated above the heaps.

By August the river was trickling upon a bed shallow and dark brown with algae. The eddies were motionless and warm, green with flannel weed, the feeding-places of strange water-beetles. When the fresh did come the contents of this and other backwaters would be pushed down and be likely to kill fish, for the dead water was saturated with carbonic acid gas.

The grilse had existed for nearly four months above Humpy Bridge, in an area of water half as big as a tennis court and varying in depth from two inches to three feet. Every inch of the bottom was lit up in the midday sunlight, but the fish was not visible. At dawn the prisoner thrust herself far under the roots of an alder. Once I waded in and stroked her back, but she did not move. Was she transfixed by terror? Or dulled by the long weary wait until the fall of the year, her season to spawn? Did she know me, as the harmless feeder of the trout? Already the fatal whitish-yellow fungus had spread over her head and corrupted the tail-fin. She breathed in gulps unevenly. It may have been anthropomorphic nonsense, but I thought of Isolde.

One morning, as I looked over the parapet before throwing the first spoonful, I saw below me a strange fish. Peering through my glass, I saw the clove-marks of a pug, as netsmen called a peal which had survived many spawnings, and returned each time to clean itself in the sea. Unlike most male salmon, the cock sea-trout usually recovered from the privations of prolonged waiting in fresh water.

At twilight, as the bats began to flitter over the water, the great pug sinuated slowly from its refuge, and hovered a while just under the surface. Sometimes the rusty back-fin idled out. It was joined by the grilse, which hovered beside it. As the moon lifted over the spruce firs on the hill the pug turned, pushing a wave as it ripped downstream. It rolled like a porpoise, showing a gleam of silver-gold and brown; then it leapt, to fall back with a splash that could be heard for a hundred yards or more. It was followed by the grilse. The two fish returned and hovered again, side by side; then they drove downstream again, the pug turning on its side, showing the taper and thickness of its body, as it rubbed head and flank with a flapping movement on the river-bed. Afterwards the listlessness of low warm water came upon it again, and it sank down, guarded by its senses of sight, hearing and smell. The grilse lay two lengths ahead of the pug.

Later, when the water ran colder, and night was come, and large moths were visible in the light of the moon overhead, the pug leapt again. Then it drove up to the shallows, to lie in the run, just behind the grilse, to breathe water made alive by oxygen absorbed from every bubble of rock-blow on the river's way down from the moor.

On the bank above the pool, where the foxhunter's horses, out to summer grass, came to drink and ruffle the gravel with their bright iron shoes at noon, something moved dimly. It was a sheep, lying on its side. It had wandered down from the hills, where the shepherd had not seen its condition. The dreaded blowfly had struck, and scores of maggots had hatched upon its fleece, all in one hot day. By the end of the second day of affliction the woolly animal was in full torment. Wasps, which nested upon the river bank, seeking during the day meat for their queen grubs, had for the moment left the prostrate animal, but the blow-fly maggots were still working with restless fever for pupation. By the smell, the ewe had been treated with a solution of carbolic acid; but the green and blue flies had returned, and within an hour or two a new battalion of ivory-sweaty maggots were tunnelling between hide and flesh. The shepherd worked early and late, but was not so strong as the sun, which must have appeared as a benevolent god to land-flies that year. How innocent, by comparison, were the frail and selfless ephemeral flies of the river, with their sealed mouths!

The sheep kicked convulsively; the odours of corruption arose with the damp air moving down the valley. Drifting down the valley came the delicious smell of honey, with a memory, for me, of yellow wax tapers burning in Pyrenean churches. The summer had been kind to the bees; many swarms from hive and skep had travelled away and become wild. There were three nests under the wooden superstructure of the viaduct, over which the trains rolled, bringing visitors to the Atlantic coast.

The older children had wanted me to smoke out the wasps as soon as they had found the nests, each under its tuft of grass, with a rough entrance about the size of a penny; but it was thought best to wait until night, when the wasps' wings would be limp. The elder boy, out of earshot of the two smaller ones, was promised that he would be awakened in time to see the fun.

At eleven o'clock, with Scorpio flashing red-gemmeous over the tree-tops, we set out. I wondered, a little sadly, if I had such enthusiasm for so little when I was young. The sky gleamed with a pallid blue above the dark fir plantation on the high ground north-west. Oaks and beeches in the deer park seemed to be filled with a bluish-black power of mysterious night-life. Crossing the ornamental bridge we could just see the glimmer of trout rings by the bend of the river where the shrunken run moved now so quietly into the pool. A late train rumbled over the viaduct. A heron by the Peal Stone Falls, disturbed by the dilating play of flame on steam, cried harshly and flew down-river to pitch within three yards of our motionless selves, to walk slowly to the verge of the water—and to shriek with terror as it flapped up so near our faces.

The river murmured over the shallows. A long-eared owl called with its short note among the spruces behind the cottage. Now for it! A match was struck, held shakily while wasp after wasp crept from the hole with sleepy hostility. At last the fusee, Victorian relic, spluttered. A reddish point of light glowed dully, falteringly. Another match, and with firm hissing it gave off its sulphurous vapours. Quick, thrust the fusee into the hole, then the clatt of turf on top, to be thrust down with the heel!

Then the other nest.

Silence in the valley, only the murmur of the river.

We went home slowly through thickening dimmit-light, the boy wide-eyed as he looked at the strange tree-shapes, asking in a whisper if they were 'mighty forest monarchs', and wondering what the nests would look

Water Play

like on the morrow. I lingered behind, and waiting on the bridge, saw a ghost moving in the water below, pale, phosphorescent—the maiden fish still there, enduring while fungus ate flesh, waiting, it seemed, with faith, with hope, to fulfil her life; to find immortality through her instinctive self-sacrifice for the future of the species. The form glimmered in the water, it moved slowly up to the run. The big sea-trout had gone. Perhaps a gaff had snatched it out, or the stab of a four-tined fork; or an otter had driven it back to deeper water above the sawmills weir.

We were out early. A few wasps hovered dejectedly by the half-charred turves pressed upon the entrance holes. They were the workers which, for various causes—such as drunkenness or gluttony in pursuit of their duties in bringing back food for the grubs—had remained out too late to return home. They buzzed valiantly but ineffectually about my ears as I struck the mattock in the turf and lifted out the first nest.

It was about the size of a football, flimsy, greyish-brown, lichen-like, and easily broken by its own weight of tiers of white grubs and asphyxiated wasps. The tiers, or sections of comb, were brittle. Each tier had its eggs, miniature grubs, growing grubs, sealed pupae and wasps about to hatch. Adult wasps, their stings protruding, lay in still attitudes between the combs. Others were dead in the act of feeding the grubs, curiously life-like as they remained half-in the cells.

The vapour of sulphur dioxide had caught the nurses as they had thought of their charges before themselves. Were they females which were not barren, although not fecund like the queen their mother? For a few of the

workers can lay eggs, although they have not been ferti-
lized by a male; and these eggs hatch into males, which are
stingless and of no value to the community.

The lowest tier of the nest was the smallest, the most
recently made from wood-cement champed and mixed by
the jaws of the workers. Here lay a wasp larger than any
other. Three large wasps, her daughters, lay by her head.
They faced her, bowed in death. She was the queen who,
alone, had sought the mouse-hole in the bank, enlarged it,
cemented its roof, constructed the original hexagon cells,
to lay an egg in each, feed the larvae, watch them seal
themselves below white silken caps when they were
grown, and later, stroke their antennae to encourage them
as they bit their way out, wan and languid, to become
daughter-helpers, the princesses.

I opened some of the sealed cells. Within were wasps in
embryo, white as ivory, fragile with eyes growing a pale
brown. In one cell was an impostor, a brown and black
insect looking like a bee, whose parent had crept into the
nest and laid an egg in a cell beside a wasp egg; and when
the impostor had hatched, it had eaten the wasp egg, and
then food from a gentle nurse; and but for disaster and
death, the impostor would creep out and fly away to lay
eggs in other nests, and so continue the line of impostors
called ichneumon flies.

With the nest on a shovel, I went to the top arc of the
bridge, and began to pull the grubs out of the cells and drop
them into the water. Some of them were still alive, champ-
ing their jaws hungrily, as they fell swirling in the stream
below. A greenish dull flash, and a Loch Leven trout had
risen. Other flashes. Soon the water was breaking as each
grub touched the surface. Grubs, pupae, young wasps—up

the trout rolled for the manna dropping from heaven. The Clown, who had moved into deeper water, waited exactly below where they fell.

I stood there until midday, while several thousand grubs went over the parapet. I grew tired of the meticulous work of separating each grub from its cell, and began to drop wads of them over. The Clown rolled up in half-turns as before. He was watching each fragment as it fell straight down. I became bored with him, and went back for a shovelful of dead wasps. Would the formic acid in their stings kill him? I did not care. My fingers were messy, and smelled of old fireworks.

The Clown trout took more than three hundred. To-morrow, I thought, I shall see him upended in the shallows. But when I went there the next day and peered over, he came up and looked at me, as though waiting for more.

The pool was black; the three runs, passing under the arches of the bridge and over the rugged spillways scarcely stirred its surface. When would rain come? I dreaded *forunculosis*, a plague which sometimes came in warm water and killed salmon as the black death killed men and women in the Middle Ages. When would the purging rains come?

Spate

I was suddenly awake, and listening. The low roar from the falls was more remote. Then I realized that it was being deflected by a thousand drops falling upon leaves, flowers and tree-branch outside my open window. I got out of bed and listened. The fringe of thatch was not yet dripping; the rain fell softly; it was *suent* rain; soft, gentle, warm, gracious. My spirit felt freedom, new life came into me as I stood there listening for the noises of wind, for the roar of the south-west bringing upon the land Atlantic bombards to shed their liquor. The night was starless dark. I stood by the casement, imagining days and nights of steady rain, to drain into the marshes and the bogs of the moor, to sink through peat, through cracks in beds of clay and rock, to run forth as spring-water, to feed the runners to swell the brooks tributary to the river and so down the valley which had one of the best beats in the West Country, above the Junction Pool. There the river added its water to big brother Taw which in the estuary joined with sister Torridge, the Celtic waters flowing together to the sea, bearing the dripped clouds from the inner watersheds of two moors which were the cloud barriers between Severn Sea and Cornwall.

Thinking of the fish, my imagination seeing them in the

river outside, I could not sleep, but lay listening to the steady beat of rain. How heavy was it? My electric torch revealed silver lattices parallel with the oaken casement uprights. I did not need to sleep, I was happy, floating in thoughts of jaded salmon beginning to roll around their stagnant pools, upon whose luminous roofs struck the hammers of the rain. I could sense the excitement in fish and animal and bird at imminent change and movement: new hope for salmon, food for resident trout and eels, variety and change and adventure for all along the water courses.

Soon after dawn I was awake and dressed and out, opening my garden gate just as the light of an oil-lamp began to shine in the cottage of one of the estate carpenters down the lane. The wind had swept across the deer park and stripped many of the leaves from the limes; now it had almost dropped, leaving plashes of rain in rut and pothole, and the river risen only two inches above the dried and bleached flannel weed on exposed rocks and alder roots. Risen not with rock-water from the springs, but from road drains; water unclear and foul. It had put down every trout and salmon and parr below its dullness. It was warm; it floated away on top of the streams, gradually absorbing oxygen as it was flung about in run and over fall. Even so, it was useless water. The fish waited for it to pass away, before life could come to them again.

I returned to the cottage, to shave and have my cold tub; then I went out again, to see the lifeless road-and-drain water, with its false rainbows of oil, still moving sluggishly down. Back again, for breakfast at the long oak table; but where was the second boy?

Spate

Most sympathetic and understanding, this child often accompanied me in my riverside inspections. Several times during the hot weather I had observed him standing in valiant attitude as he gazed upwards, to shout in his treble voice, 'God! Send down rain! God!! SEND DOWN RAIN!!'

Sometimes he had been critical about the non-fulfilment of his demands on my behalf; but in tones that were of innocence itself.

The door opened, and the small, almost demure child came in. He said quietly, 'God has sent down that rain.'

'But it's not a proper spate.'

'But it *is* a proper spate.'

'A spate is something much more than mere road washings.'

'Big high 'normous spate!' His cheeks were faintly pink.

Hand in hand we hastened out of the house. A few steps beyond the iron gates I saw the swirling gleam of water. The river had risen two feet and more. So I apologized to John, adding that I wished I had remained, for I had never seen the wall of water, akin to the Severn bore, coming down this river, the head of a true spate. It must have plunged down, a new river replacing the old with a dozen or more times the old river's volume, with exhilarating violence. The plunging water was a thick brown colour, heavy with leaves, sticks and other scavengings. Gone was the old stick-heap on the middle pier of the bridge, torn off, swept away. The level was rising fast as we stood there. Amidst frothing scum the flotsam of leaves, twigs, bottles, tins and hen's feathers crept in little undulations over the drowning grasses of the bank.

Where the pit of one of the burnt-out wasps' nests had

been was an eddy in which bubbles revolved about a corked and empty medicine bottle. On the gravel-ridges the docks and water-celery plants were washed flat and clogged with layers of dead leaves, like old-fashioned bills stuck on an iron spike in a merchant's office.

After breakfast we returned. The alders were now rising out of water which had spread into the deer park. Within twenty-four hours, I thought, sea-trout from the ocean would be boring through green-grey glissades curving over the falls below the arches of the bridge.

The energy of the water and the roar in the air drew me, with my little companion, many times to see the spate. At eleven o'clock it reached its height, then the water began to drop back. It was fining down quickly. I could distinguish new leaves from fragments of old leaves as they were borne down and twirled over the stones of the now-visible gravel above the bridge. Grasses which had been drowned at ten o'clock were, by midday, exposed and drooping with a fine brown silt, a foot above the river level. Young celery plants and docks on the gravel verges were bowed with their loads of water-weed and other plants' leaves. On one of the lower branches of an alder a young jackdaw was hanging. Already a green spanish fly was examining the corpse; while the broad-arrows of a heron's clawed feet were imprinted on the sandy scour left below the hole that once had held a wasps' nest.

Here the child, who in the sun had gravely removed his clothes, knelt in absorption to realize some dream in the new sand. I watched the scrapings and scoopings of his hands, actions which to him were the building of a farm-yard. That was a hayrick, that a cattle shippen, that was Farmer's bullock dog, Towser——

Spate

And that!—just beside his toes, not a yard away from where he knelt, was the grilse rolling out of the water. The boy was startled, and said 'Cor darn!', which he had heard from the farmer occupying the lodge, and looked at me with round eyes. We laughed together, it seemed somehow to be funny. We waited for another laugh; but when the fish did not come again, we went up the river to the Peal Stone Falls, and waited below the white water, hoping to see peal jumping there. We went to look after luncheon, and again saw nothing. All during the drought, in the mouths of the Two Rivers thirty-six licensed nets, each two hundred yards long, had been sweeping the shallow estuary eight out of every twenty-four hours all through the summer, for fish which ran up with every flowing tide and down again with every lapsing tide except during the week-ends.

I was hoping to take the small peal, which came in schools from the sea—fish of all sizes up to a pound—on a new hackled fly I had tied and dressed myself. It had a yellow worsted body enwound with gilt wire. I had killed brown trout with it, while fishing upstream in the comparatively slow, stained water above the falls. Fish after fish, waiting there, a foot from the rushy bank, had sucked it in, quietly. They were waiting for beetles, crane-flies, bees, perhaps even wasps, I thought. My yellow-bodied fly fell before them, they were barblessly hooked, pressure on the line kept the curved steel in their jaws, they were in the net. It was excellent water; the Peal Stone was covered, the freshet was fining down; but not one school peal in the river.

I went down to Steep Weir after tea, and saw the reason. Someone had shut the fender of the fish-pass and spiked it down with six-inch nails driven into holes bored by an auger in the oak side-posts.

Had the miller done this, to conserve water during the drought? I remembered what the agent had said about the grist mill below the weir. The wooden wheel was old, in need of replacement; a small oil-engine put in would cost no more than a new wheel, to work the stones which ground barley into pig-meal for farmers.

Moved by the sight of many peal jumping vainly out of bashing waters on the rock below—fish of all sizes being up-ended and thrown about—I climbed down into the walled spillway below the fender, and examined a jet of water spurting between two of the big, faced stones. Once, the rectangular blocks had been mortared; now, most of the mortar was gone. How firm was the walling? How much strength was needed to shift one of the blocks, so that the spurt became a gush, washing the hole larger until the wall was breached, and, in a heavier spate, the entire dam collapsed?

Appalled by the thought, I withdrew; to return, thinking that there could be no harm in seeing if the faced-stones were loose. I inserted the bar; they were firm, to my relief.

The agent had told me that orders had been given that the fender must be left open when the mill was not working, so I had no hesitation in helping the miller to do his duty. I returned for hacksaw, hammer and cold chisel; and when I left, the water was pouring under the fender, and no more fish vainly trying to get up the weir.

Had I been moved on their behalf, or my own? I can say this truthfully: I now cared more for the fish than for fishing.

I Behold the Hebrides

At the beginning of September my wife and I packed a kitbag and small tent, and with rods, candle-lanthorn, frying-pan, kettle, blankets and ground-sheet, early one morning set out for North Britain in the Silver Eagle. In those days the roads were not congested, and the driver in an open sports car, wearing leather coat, goggles and flying helmet, would greet another like himself with enthusiasm; and if he were going the same way as himself, usually a dust-up occurred. My engine was a six-cylinder job, with three carburetters, and capable of 4,800 r.p.m., or eighty miles an hour—quite a speed for a 1930 model. Driving was an adventure, hedges rushed past, the grey road with them, and many a corner appeared suddenly, to test the road-holding. The headlights were good, throwing converging beams a thousand feet ahead, and dipping to the left at a flick of the switch on the steering column. I felt pride that my motor-car was the same model that had raced the Blue Train, from the Riviera to Calais, beating it by an hour and a half.

We went by way of Taunton, Bristol, Gloucester and Coventry, at which town I called at the works to have the timing checked and the carburetters synchronized. This

I Behold the Hebrides

being done, we went on, taking it easy, and spent the night at Blackpool, to enjoy the illuminations, the crowds and the sideshows. We swished down spiral chutes around tall towers on coconut mats, leaving our entrails nightmarishly behind us; plunged from great heights in flat-bottom'd boats, which leapt in splashing bounds over the lake below; we entered ghostly houses, saw performing dwarfs, fleas, animals and ladies both bearded and tattoo'd—and returning to our boarding house at 11 P.M., ate the national-industrial supper of fried fish and chips.

The next morning we left for Lancaster and Kendall, and the long road rising to Shap Fell, entering a high wild land where the curlew glided on hooped wings; and so to Penrith, and the fast stretch to Carlisle, whereon an average of sixty was held. A stop for some beer, and postcards sent to the children in Devon, then the left fork to the border, Gretna, and Scotland the brave! I was in the land of my fathers for the first time, speaking the word Ecclefechan like a native, and so to the cobbled, foggy and dour streets of industrial Glasgow; and passing through without stopping, we opened up along the road to Helensburgh, and for miles of slower motoring beside water to Garelochhead, and on past Loch Long to Loch Fyne, following the road above the western bank to Inverary, with its ducal castle and fishing nets drying on poles by the waterside. Our eyes were now looking for a camping place for the night. The boat for the Hebrides did not leave until the next afternoon, and it was but thirty-six miles to the port at the head of the promontory of Kintyre.

Although a little wearied by the journey, the idea of sleeping under a roof when wild woods bordered the road was scorned. We found a ride by which to enter a covert, and hiding the Silver Eagle among hazel clumps, put up the tent and made a fire of birch-bark and nut-sticks. Stones for tripod, and soon bacon and tomatoes were frying in the pan, and kettle beginning to sing. Tea drunk as one reclined on a bed of dry leaves and moss, while a small, neat fire glowed ember-red, with yellow points of hazel-wood flame, before the open end of the bivouac tent, and pipe drawing perfectly, was my idea of contentment.

When we had washed up, and packed the wicker basket, I left my wife writing a letter, and explored the wood. I came to a burn, in which were trout. Soon I was back at camp for my little rod; but the trout were small, and of the dark-bronze hue of maturity in acid water, a race of dwarfs. It was no fun taking them, so after catching four, I put them back uninjured by barbless hook, and returned to camp, recalling, with a shade of melancholy, a boyhood dream of living wild in some Scottish forest, feeding myself by skill with rod, catapult and cross-bow.

It was a fine night, our sleeping was deep, we were up at sunrise, and spent the rest of the day until the packet left for Port Ellen on the quay at Tarbert, watching among other things herring girls gutting, with knife-flicks from cloth-bound salted hands, fish at the rate of forty a minute. Down in the sea below the quay the corpses of herrings glinted blue, millions of herrings recently tipped into the water by order, to keep up market prices, in accordance with the economical ideas of those times.

The cost of taking the motor to Islay was £5, too much for our resources; so we left it in a garage at Tarbert. We recognized a fellow guest in the boat, with his black retriever, and at Port Ellen were met by our friends, and soon were having tea and bannocks at the other end of the island. The house was full, quarters had been found for us some two miles away, in a new, small, concrete villa; and after supper of cold grouse and venison, we insisted on walking to our place, under a starry sky, having arranged to be at the lodge at ten o'clock the next morning. Five miles to walk, back and forth every day? It was nothing, we preferred walking to going by car, we declared. This was not so much to save others from the fag of carting us about, as truth. What better than to flop into bed, body worked out, and find deep sleep at once?

The lodge which our friends had taken for a month was really a farmhouse, but not much farming was done, two cows only being kept for the house. Painters, naturalists and lovers of wild scenery came in the late spring and early summer; in autumn it was the turn of sportsmen. We lived on venison, black-necked pheasants and an occasional ptarmigan. We walked far over the heather; and once were rowed close to the rocks of a wild and broken shore, where thong-weed at low tide glistened in the sun, and seals with submarine eyeballs came up, just out of gunshot, to stare as though innocently at the movements atop the slow and swelling water. We were on our way by boat to avoid climbing over the headland which the ladies, one riding a white pony, were crossing on foot.

It was grand, body-hardening country. Every night we walked back under familiar stars, and returned at morning when the sun was low over the mountains of Dumfries-shire. It was no good fishing, they said, while the burn was a mere black trickle; but one afternoon I took my small rod and caught several dwarf trout on the hackle fly. It was exciting to see an occasional boil in one or other of the peat-brown pools lying between the shrunken runs. There salmon were waiting for the spate to carry them to the redds. The time of year seemed to be waiting, so quiet, so silent. Sitting amidst honey smells which had drawn wild bees to the last of the bells of the heath, I wondered if land-locked salmon felt frustration, if they were capable of realizing, in their own dim way, their plight? Were they patient? Why did some fish, running up early in the year, choose to endure such poor conditions, months before November spawning time? Why did other fish, startled or shocked, go down to the sea again, the water not being too low over the stickles? These burn fish could not escape, the flow over the gravelly shallows being only three or four inches. What were their feelings? For they had feelings, even if they were not able to think. What were those feelings? Resignation, acceptance, trust? Uneasiness and impotence? Had the inspiration which urged them into their native rivers failed, in proportion to the failing of the life-giving stream of water which they faced? Was there a spirit in the water which they obeyed instinctively? How far was the spirit of place, of environment the conditioner of creativeness? For man (as artist), bird, animal and fish? The salmon was born to die, if it survived sea and river enemies, of exhaustion after spawning, unless it could get back to salt water in time to clean itself, thereafter to charge its body anew with food. Did it run up from the sea merely for the sexual feeling of its milt or roe being shed beside a casual mate on the redds? Was it but automaton, drawn to destruction by a sensation implanted in its sexual organs? I wanted to find the secret of life, I desired to con-firm with my mind what my intuition had already told me: that animals in varying species and states of evolution were basically as human beings: that the purpose of life, as shown

in evolution, was to create beauty: that love was linked
with beauty, and linked also with what was called honour
and courage, otherwise fidelity to its own sort, or species:
that love was a main vital force, and to call it God was a
simple fact.

We walked on the ptarmigan slopes under the mountains, sometimes carrying guns, but always for the fun of
walking, and feeling the rock winds upon our faces.
There, across the sound, were the paps of Jura, and that
bird flying down a rock pipit was a merlin. The shooting
was the rough kind I was used to, walking up our own
game, the occasional hare and pheasant. Across the bogs I
shot two snipe, using No. 7 shot, a right and left and was
as surprised as were the two other guns. I did not go stalking; a stag's carcass already hung in the bothy, only part
of it eaten. What I hoped for was rain, so that I could fish
the burn. I had already explored half a mile of its course,
and favoured a certain straight length, of medium depth
of water, which flowed with just enough unevenness to
riffle the streams passing over rock strata, in which were
pits. It looked to me to be just the place where a salmon
would lie, since it resembled the water in the deer park
above the second washed-out ornamental dam, the place
where I had discovered the grilse sheltering under a cut
branch lying in the river, and taken the photographs.

The rain came on our last afternoon, while we were
having tea. I hurried outside to the high-arched bridge
over the road to see the beginning of the spate. Beneath
me the stream, narrow in a trough between two walls of
rock, fell solidly into a pool three feet below the bend of
water still the colour of whisky. That was the exact hue;

I Behold the Hebrides

I was about to make a note of it when it struck me as obvious—for the island had several clusters of white buildings where whisky was distilled from malted barley and burn water. Perhaps the cliché of *amber* would be simpler. The water fell solidly into the pool, still peat-stained; but it was rising, or rather swelling, the amber water of the pools being pushed before the spate, and lipping slightly higher against the rocks. As I watched, the water became like porter, froth being churned up in the pool with leaves and a black stick or two; then the waterfall gushed wide, covering the pool as with dirty fleeces while it roared down. I waited for some time, but saw no fish; they would begin to run when the spate was over and the water dropping back.

The rain had ceased during the past hour, and already the far white threads cascading down the mountain were diminishing. Would it be too late to fish in the morning, I wondered, as we walked back that night seeing Orion low in the south-east, sign that winter was on the way, and soon my feet would have passed upon that road for the last time in my life. It was ever so: scenes, faces, moments—always the flow of time, leaving one only the pellicles of former living. A melancholy thought; and one which might have been dispelled by a glass of amber burn water in which malted grain had been stepped, and then distilled; but in those days I was afraid of the stuff, considering that no 'artificial' stimulation was needed, unaware of the food value of whisky taken occasionally and not unsparingly.

There was more rain in the night, and the next afternoon, when the burn was only a few inches above its former level, I went fishing, having chosen my fly, a moth-spoiled Black Dog from my grandfather's japanned circu-

I Behold the Hebrides

lar iron case, which had sections under its hand-made lid
painted white, wherein feathered hooks, also hand-made
and stove-enamelled black, lay shabbily, yet somehow akin
to the water of the burn.

The eye of the Black Dog was threaded by the end of
the silk worm gut of level 2-X gauge, which had a dead-
weight breaking strain of two pounds. The gut was dark
brown, having been stained with nitrate of silver against
glint when under water. I felt that if I did not make myself
go slowly about my business of tying the correct turle
knot, and suppress a rising excitement, I would hook a fish
only to hear the reel's scream, which hitherto I had heard
only in imagination, suddenly end, as the rod ceased to
bend—my first salmon lost through haste.

Having tied the Dog, or what was left of it, to the pliant
damped gut, I went towards the water, going down on one
knee a rod's length from the bank; and drawing out line,
threw the Dog to and fro over my head, with the same
ease akin to confidence, or satisfaction in the balance of
tapered rod and tapered line, which I had felt in Canada
when fishing with the frayed Coachman. Then, loop held
ready to loosen as the fly went out for its first swim in the
burn, I lowered the rod point and the fly flipped almost
imperceptibly into the settled porter, and still on one knee,
I lifted the rod point and thought I was caught in a log.
No, it was a salmon, and in the very place I had imagined
a fish to lie, and at the first cast!

It was not very exciting, the playing of that fish. It was
small, and never jumped; it tried to bore down to the
bottom all the time. At last I stood with shortened line,
while it finally tired itself out, and slipping the net under
it, took it upon the heather, noting the pale rose-rust

tarnish upon its scales, the small head and hog-back: a summer grilse, which turned the pointer of the kitchen scales to 5 lb.

The journey home was the longest I ever made in the Silver Eagle, or in any other motor, without a relief driver. We started at dawn, and returned by the same route to Lancaster and Preston, turning off for Wigan. A year or two later, I would not have heard what I heard then—the noises of clogs on the feet of mill-girls in black shawls leaving factories at noon were as thousands of wavelets breaking on rocks. Through other grim and congested industrial towns, tediously slow, our route lay, to Chester and on down to Shrewsbury, Ludlow and Hereford, where the driver stopped to sleep on the wayside grass. Then on to Ross-on-Wye, Gloucester, Bristol, Taunton: and so home in the early hours of the next morning, the speedometer clocking 550 miles. We were both very tired indeed, though sustained by the flesh of the grilse, which had been given to us, cooked, on our departure.

As I lay sleepless in bed, with wheels turning in my head, and many scenes disintegrating before my eyes, I wondered if a salmon felt as I did, after its long journey past the hazards of the estuary, including the roar of white water in clash upon dreaded rocks. Yet the salmon endured for a purpose; I had merely forced myself upon so long a journey in order to test my powers of endurance.

Merely that? Was I not, like the salmon, coming to where my heart lay?

Nog & Co.

The green *ranunculus* weeds, instead of being torn away from precarious holdings in the gravel, as had been prophesied by more than one riparian expert in The Fisherman's Arms, were growing, and spreading the more luxuriantly with each freshet. Their leafy strings delayed the silt moving down, and so the lower stalks were buried, only to increase their holdings by cadet rootlets; and when the lusty sunshine of another West Country spring broke through Atlantic clouds, the original plants were seen to have increased a hundredfold, with more feelers seeking sunlight through the cold clear water. Bines broke off and drifted downstream, to lodge against stones and put forth cadets which were buried by sand ever in motion around the stones of the river bed. Such motion was caused by the slightest alteration; a bine, curled round a stone, started its own burial.

I was never easy in the company of the matter-of-fact type of angler I met at The Fisherman's Arms: nevertheless I went there, hopefully, several times every season, usually in the evening. On one visit I met the retired colonel in the bar. 'Hullo,' he said. 'Curious how Nature works, isn't it? A few years ago the banks of the river, right up to

Taw Marsh, were covered by jungles of balsam, higher
than a man, with pink bean-like flowers. You must have
seen 'em, because you mention 'em in *Tarka*. Some garden stray, lacking parasites no doubt. Now we're beginning to get an abundance of green weed in the water.
I've been fouled again and again with the beastly stuff this
season. I suppose it arrived on a heron's foot.'
  'I've seen a good many herons about.'
  'Too many, in my opinion. But you fellows with what
I call the taint don't like the idea of shedding blood, do
you? If I had my way I'd shoot the lot.'

Herons regularly flew up the river to fish my water.
They arrived in succession, from one sunrise to another,
from midsummer onwards. Each heron had its particular
standing place. Some were common to all. Like the trout
taking its stance in the stream where the food was most
plentiful, so the heron stood in shallow water on a jut of
mossy rock at the tail of an eddy, where the trout awaited
hatching nymphs.
  I became accustomed to seeing ash-grey wings flapping up almost as soon as I lifted, with its rusty noise, the
iron latch of the deer park gate. My Loch Levens had been
marked down by glassy eyes.
  That would never do. Behind an oak tree, with my spy-
glass, I lay in wait. A heron flew up the river, planed
down, pitched, looked around, then began to walk to the
water. It saw me, and up it tumbled into air.
  The next bird to arrive, probably a fledgeling of that
year, was more direct. It landed on the bank, and walked
into shallow water, there to stand and await the return of
fingerling trout and fry which had been scared away by

previous wings soaring up and away. After a few minutes the fish were evidently back: through my glass I saw the yellow beak snick out with lightning thrusts. I yelled in anger.

Why, I thought unreasonably, didn't the damned herons fish the estuary, where fish could be taken, in that wide place of sandbank and shelving water streams, without mutual anxiety? Worms in the mud-banks—some of them covering deposits of black oak leaves—fed many flat-fish, called flukes, as well as small bass, crabs and shrimps—enough food for all. Herons did fish there, of course, no doubt claiming territory. The young birds flying up my river were dispossessed birds, driven away by parents, and forced to be pioneers.

Day after day, heron after heron, at intervals of an hour or so, came up the river and stood motionless in shallow water at the edge of the pool where the Clown, now bigger than the largest Loch Leven, was lying.

How had the invasion come about? Probably young birds had followed their parents, who had turned on them. Birds and mammals learn by imitation. What parental curses had come from yellow beaks, on moonlit nights, and in the clarity of dawns spreading over the moor? Old Nog, and memories of five hundred dollars, had some claim on me; but his relations were another kettle of fish.

When next I fed my fish, I saw that many smaller wild brownies and parr, which previously had joined my school that term, were missing. And one morning, having startled a heron that shrieked to see me, when I looked over the bridge there was the Clown moving very slowly to the comparatively deeper water by the floating alder roots. Upon the back of his head was a strange bluish mark.

Peering down through my glass, I saw that the pate had been pierced in two places, the wounds being three-quarters of an inch apart.

The Clown did not arrive to feed with the others when I broadcast the next spoonfuls. The following morning, when I went out, two herons flew up. I got my shriek in first this time; and hastening to the river, saw their excited toe-prints on the sandy scour just above the deeper water under the western arch. On the stones below one of the Loch Levens was lying on its side. Next day the herons were there again. My best Loch Leven, a pound-and-a-half fish, lay half in the water, with marks as of shears pressed on its head and again on its flanks. One of the birds had seized it, and apparently failed to swallow it.

I kept further watch, and learned that about nine herons were fishing all day and most of the night along my beat. I went to see the agent, and asked permission to carry a gun along the river. The agent in due course spoke to the Lord of All, who said that I might shoot one, or two.

Meanwhile the Clown fed no more with the other fish. He was beat. He grew thinner. His wound spread into a black patch from his head down towards his tail. Once when he drifted down directly under the bridge, I thought that he was becoming blind. Would he starve to death? I had read, in *Where the Bright Waters Meet*, lent to me by the judge at The Fisherman's Arms, of old blind trout, turning black with starvation. Could I seal the Clown up in the eel trap? Or keep him in the Clay Pit, and dangle food before his neb?

The children were put to collect slugs and snails from the garden. I dropped some before him, as he reposed under the eastern arch of the bridge. He ate some of the slugs, and seemed a little less unlively afterwards. Could he see? Did he smell them?

He took up his quarters under that arch. One of the big Loch Levens had lived there, but I pushed it out with a stick. Then I tried to lure it back, as a guard to the Clown. It returned, so did my doubts. Would it act as a decoy? I chased it out again, and put the eel-trap under the arch; to see next morning, with satisfaction, that the Clown had taken up residence. Let any heron try and get him out of that iron mask, I thought.

When I saw one wading at the edge of the run at the bend above the bridge, I bought a box of No. 4 shot cartridges; and put my plan into action. Going to Humpy Bridge, I waited until I saw gliding grey wings pitch below the Peal Stone Falls and then returned for something with which I strolled up the path through the wooded hill behind my cottage, carrying it under my jacket. It was in three parts, and therefore in the eyes of the law did not need a licence.

From the top of the hill, at the west end, I had, as it were, a heron's eye view. My thoughts were heron thoughts as I walked on towards the viaduct, where, leaving the fir trees, I descended upon steep scree which had been tipped down the hillside to strengthen the foundations of the first pillar supporting the span of iron and wood which carried the railway line nearly two hundred feet above the valley.

For the first time I was going to walk down the river without having first walked up. Moreover, I was going to walk down on the *right* bank. My particular destination was the Peal Stone Falls, where the noise of plunging water would overlay any noise of my approach. I felt nervous as

I drew near, having fitted barrels, stock and cover-piece together. There was a sqwark, and a shock that was mutual. I fired one barrel wildly; the other less so; the heron collapsed into feathers, loose neck and shambled legs. I disliked what I had done, and was tremulous.

After being skinned, its body was boiled in a copper fish-kettle, the flesh put through a mincing machine, and made into fish-balls, which were then dropped into the water of the eastern arch, so that fragments went into the eel trap, now known as Clown Castle. The occupant took them slowly at first, then with more agility.

A few days later another heron, surprised by an apparent reversal of the earth's orbit, fell down dead with shock. Its rissoles lasted four more days. When I hauled out the Clown he looked better. The slide through the grass, wetted for his sinuation, seemed to stimulate him, despite a long dark thread hanging from his gut. I had read of this parasitical worm in one of the quarterly Salmon and Trout Association magazines, a complete set of which I had bought from Dr. Price-Tannatt, a fellow-member of the Association, and one of the authorities on the Salmonidae.

The intestinal parasite was possibly one of the causes of the loss of condition, but Clown had also been badly hurt by the gripping power of the heron's beak. The scales were broken, the skin bruised, the flesh contused. I wondered if it would be possible to give him a purgative, a vermicide, perhaps a dose of Epsom salts, to clear his gut; but let him go back to his element. Clown, back in water, rushed about when a shower of bucket food descended, and soon lost the black thread, as I saw through my glass when he appeared with other fish for the daily diet. Whether the heron-flesh had acted as a vermicide, I do not know; but in time the dark stain on his back gave way to a golden brown and once more he was the show-piece among my dependants.

Both the herons were young birds. Old Nog was still alive. I recognized him by his cracked and particularly raucous voice; and by the way he flew up when I was at least twenty gunshots from him, although I carried the gun no more.

One Sunday afternoon, while sitting in the shade of an ash tree near the pool below Boundary Bridge, I heard what I thought to be a horse walking in the river, plunging about; and sitting still, was surprised to see two otters coming down, wrestling and apparently fighting. They were playing. They rolled and dived, and beat their long tapered tails, which made the plunging noises.

One ran out beside the river and turning on its back on a gravel bank drove its pate into the stones, getting up to do it again and again. Through my spy-glass I saw a white bead on its brow, and recognized this as a tick, having seen a similar parasite on a tame otter some years before. The tick was a quarter of an inch in diameter, and remained there despite the rubbing. By the broad pate the otter was a dog. Across the river appeared the sleek bulrush-brown head of the bitch, with an eel in her mouth. She drew herself upon the rock, and chewed it tail first. Over to her, in a series of loops, leapt the dog, dashing himself at her, and hauling her by the rudder into the water. The plunging began again, and continued downriver among the willow islets.

I was about to get up when I heard the noises coming back again; and looking in the pool, I saw that they had been joined by two young otters. Then appeared a third, and a fourth. The broader-headed dog dashed at them, and they played together in the pool, the bitch joining in. At one time they followed each other, the dog leading, swimming up to bob out of the water while the cub behind him was diving under again, porpoise-like. This bobbing and diving continued, one following closely behind the other, until the effect of a coiling serpent was made. I wondered if the fabulous Loch Ness Monster had been a family of otters playing like this.

Then they disappeared. Perhaps they had winded me, and had sunk away, leaving only nostrils out of water under the bank; or gone down the stickle underwater, brown and smooth as ribbon-weed, keeping themselves just a little faster than the water by paddling with their webbed front feet, touching down over the stones in slow motion, as I had seen otters swimming under rapid shoaling water when in my youth I had followed hounds upon the banks of Taw, Torridge, Tavy, Teign—the *ta* of the Celts, meaning water, *a* being the diminutive; a theory (by no means accepted by all philologists) of which I was ignorant when, suddenly, the otter of my imagination named himself tarka—wandering as water, the little water-wanderer, tarka of the Celts, who were before the Romans, the Vikings, the Saxons and the Normans.

During my first year in the valley, the forester of the estate had told me that otters bred, early every spring, in the large stick-pile lodged on rock beside the Wheel Pool, where the water turned slowly in an open cavern worn by its own circumfluence. Thinking to dislodge them, to send them to another breeding place, I had removed the sticks, during several days; and when they were dried, we had a bonfire one night, the embers of which were still red under white ash the next morning. Now, as I sat beside the Wheel Pool, I wondered if the pair had gone upriver, the bitch to lay her cubs in some holt in the roots of a tree.

And thinking of otters, I remembered Arthur Heinemann, an eccentric sporting character on Exmoor in my young days—perhaps the last of the Victorian wild men of the West Country—who wrote in *The Field* and other papers under the name of *Peep-Out*. Arthur told me that once he came upon a bitch otter sunning herself on a rock, with three dog otters lying around her, also sunning themselves. It was clicketting time, and by the relaxed attitudes of all four animals there was no jealousy; but whether the bitch had the one mate, while the two odd-dogs out were in agreement as spectators, the bitch having chosen her cubs' sire (she the queen, he the courtier waiting on her favours, as in the natural world where human tensions of the mind are unknown) Arthur did not say. He knew a great deal about otters, and when he hunted them alone, he did so with one and a half couple of hounds, often at night, and be damned he said, to barriers of stirring, iron-shod poles across the stickles, to turn the hunted beast. He let his hounds do the hunting, he the advisor. He was an American-Jew, a cousin of William Heinemann the London publisher, and had carried the horn of the Eton College Beagles in the 'nineties. Later, he became a Master of the Cheriton Otter Hounds. I found him always a sensitive, knowledgeable and delightful companion.

Arthur Heinemann privately hunted otters; and was greatly attached to a tame bitch called Louie. He had also a tame badger, which was devoted to him—a rare thing, for while an otter makes a delightful pet, a badger is usually uncertain, and liable to bite most savagely the hand that caresses it.

But not Arthur's Brockie. One morning he missed it, and wondered where it had gone; and later a farmer rode up to the farmhouse on the moor where Arthur lived and said, 'I've a-got thaccy Brockie, I vancy. Twad in one o' me gins in the 'aidge.' When Arthur got to the hedge, which was an earth bank topped with beech, he saw his tame badger, with its paw in a rabbit trap, and crying, he told me, piteously.

Uusually a dog in a gin, in those days of rabbits, was a tricky thing to set free: the best way was to get a two-tined fork, the kind used for pitching sheaves, with a long handle, and pin to earth the ring of the trap to which the chain was attached. This confined the trapped animal; while pressure on the spring with stout stick or mattock, usually snapped at by the dog in its fear, released the serrated jaws. Brockie, Arthur Heinemann told me, stood still while his master opened the steel jaws and when the animal was free it stood upon its hind legs and hid its face against his knees, like a small child, whimpering.

Arthur Heinemann was one of several old-type Bohemian sporting characters, immigrants to the West Country, who were uprooted, or more often rootless, men. They were escapists, wild men who turned day into night; and sometimes liquor into food; more often than not living by mortgage and moneylender, and coming, sooner or later, to what was called among those who lived rooted lives, a bad end. The fundamental love that a man needs in his life, if he is to have steady spiritual ease is the love of place where he was a child, and first became aware of the light, and the objects which the light illumined. Did Arthur Heinemann seek, in the loneliness of Nature, what he lacked among ordinary men? It is the hurt child become man that seeks the wilderness, wherein to rebuild himself. Certainly Arthur Heinemann had a power of love over wild animals, which may have grown, if not blossomed, out of a wasted aspect of the child's life. He died, a poor man, in Taunton Infirmary.

Returning down the river bank on that Sunday afternoon on my way back to the cottage, I had a persistent feeling that the otters would be sporting in their old pool, the Wheel. When I got there I saw the gravel was kicked about; a trout-tail lay on a stone. Just above the Wheel, the wreckage of a slashed and torn salmon lay at the edge of the Fireplay. Fish scales were here among the disturbed dry gravel, too, small scales off trout. I looked for signs and scriddicks of my big fish, the Loch Leven, but found none; and climbing the nailed alder, the barked branches of which bore the marks where my shoes had pressed on hundreds of occasions, I looked down into the water and saw not one fish. I hurried on home, and came back with food-bucket and spoon; hardly had I reached for the first branch when I saw, to my relief, that most of the trout were in position in the glide below me. But now that the otters knew they were there, would they not clear out the lot?

I went back for my rod, not really wanting to fish; and returned without bothering to put on waders; I was already in my old river togs. I crossed the bridge, meaning to walk on the right bank up to the Fireplay.

With mixed feelings I threw a Tarka Twilight, with its

body of heron's crest bound by gilt tinsel and hackles of red gamecock, its whisks of pheasant's tail. It was over-greased. It flopped down upon the water, a bad cast. I had a prevision when I dropped in the fly that I would hook the big fish, and so it happened: at once I knew, by the slow repeated tuggings on my rod, that it was the Loch Leven. Had he responded to the known figure of his patron upon the bank? What treachery was this? Where was the skill in throwing a fly into a stew-pond? Had the river been a foot higher, had this been a three-pound sea-trout, able to dash fifty or a hundred yards downstream and take me with it, or break the 4-X gut, it might have been a sporting occasion. This fish had known no life other than in a pool, waiting to be fed. It bored and bored, and when it was tired it allowed itself to be drawn slowly in, on its side, and the net put under it. On the stones it lay, the barbless hook in the corner of its bony mouth. And how thin it was: it had lost a pound since being put in. Or was it female, and growing slender for spawning? What should I do? Put it back? How could I kill an old friend?

At that moment of indecision I heard the plunging noises echoing from under the big oak above. I kneeled still, and the two otters, wrestling as before, came splashing into the pool. Soundlessly they disappeared, sinking away, drifting downstream, slowly under the skin of the shallow water, modulating themselves to the gravel.

What to do with the gaping fish? Put back, it would be languid for some time. The otters would catch it easily. I opened the spike on my penknife and killed it.

The passing of the otters seemed to have stimulated the fish in the pool, for slow, contented rings began to appear: deep wimpling rings, just below the surface. Could nymphs

be swimming up at this hour? Something was being taken
under the surface: the rings were slight bulges. I flipped
over my fly and it sank, being wet, and was taken. This
happened three times; then the rise ceased, leaving me with
three other Loch Levens to lay beside the big fish; and
with these in the creel, I walked home, with wilderness
feelings, to show my catch.

'What lovely fish! What is that one, a peal at last? How
splendid!'

I explained, adding, 'I don't want to eat any of them.'

'I saw the Lord of All yesterday, and he said to me, "We
never get any trout nowadays." He said that all the fishing
was let, except the bit above the sawmills, and none of his
guests or sons fished. Why not take them to the house?'

'You don't think it's too late?'

The house was in darkness, the drive shaded by trees
and the night. I hesitated, before windows star-lit in complete silence; then sought for a small side door, hoping that
it would answer to a bell, open to receive my basket of
fish and compliments, and close again, leaving me free in
darkness.

I peered and touched, struck matches, and at last found
a door, and a bell pull. Shrill clangours filled corridors
within, stone-flagged, judged by the resonance; and when
the echoes had died away, there were footfalls, quick and
light; rattle of chain, working of bolts, creaking of key;
light. A small boy stood there, peering out.

'Be 'ee there, surenuff?'

'I have brought some trout for his Lordship's breakfast,
and will you take them, and give them to the housekeeper.'

'They'm all tu bade! What ought I tew du, do 'ee
knaw?'

'Put them on a stone floor, and tell the chef in the morning. Say they were sent by Mr. Williamson. Good night!'

'Aw, don't 'ee go, zur! Maybe I ought to tell the gentry you'm come?'

'No, I don't want to disturb them.'

'Aw, they ban't to bade! They be sittin' up still. I'd bestways tell'm, don't 'ee reckon?'

And before I could say nay, the boy, who certainly showed initiative, had gone away down the passage, leaving me, creature of wetness and ephemeral ideas, to await bigger bolts being shot, longer chains rattled, larger keys turned, a taller door opening for a welcome as though a visit on Sunday night at half-past ten o'clock by an eccentric literary tramp, his old broken shoes tied with sisal string, half-filled with gravel, and oozing water upon the Aubusson carpet had long been expected. My self-doubts became certainties, despite the graciousness of my reception: it was one of those off-days when one did everything wrong, out of suppressed intention. In vain I thought that John Middleton Murry had been tutor here round about 1910, to spend some of his time shooting trout in the river with a revolver, in intervals of instructing a younger son in the art of composing Greek iambics. My wife, as usual, took an equitable view of this new gaucherie.

'I think you were very kind to take the fish, and I am sure they will think so, too.'

'What, at half-past ten on a Sunday night?'

The next morning I had a sore throat, and later a temperature. The throat turned septic. A day or so later, as I lay in bed, my landlord—or rather old landlord, for the estate had been handed over to the heir—rode up the path before the cottage on his black horse. I heard the sedate clop of hooves, and raising myself on an elbow, saw the slight, aloof figure coming to a halt. My wife went to speak to him, he gave her an envelope and what looked like a jar. After some talk, which caused her cheeks to blush with pleasure, for she was fond of the old man, whose character she divined beneath his shyness, the hoof-falls of the black horse receded.

The Lord of All had gone out of his way to bring the invalid some jelly. With the jar was a letter asking if, when I was better, I would be so good as to teach his grandson, who was home from school, to fish with the dry fly.

Sometimes when perched at the top of the alder over-looking the Fireplay, hidden among green leaves, I had been an involuntary witness of a family scene, as mother and father trotted past, followed by their three children, on the way to teach the young entry to jump their ponies over a rushy ditch across the meadow near the viaduct. The boy jumped sometimes with arms folded; and when later he came to watch how the dry fly was worked, and I carried him from one side of the river to the other, he held himself upright by the grip of his thighs only, his hands held to his sides as though I were a pony. His balance, too, was automatic, so that, apart from the pincer-like grip below my ribs, he seemed without weight.

He came with his cousin, a boy from the north of England, who had a broader, more powerful head. He was, I fancied, not a Celt like myself, but a Norman, one whose nature required results rather than impressions. The fish were either not rising, or I could not catch any; the cat-like feeling was gone from me; I was unable to hold my audience, or part of it. I tried in several runs, but was clumsy. Then the North Country boy saw a tin riding down on the water and started a cock-shy. Soon spouts were rising as the rusty object bobbled down the runs. We looked for other things in the jetsam heaps of freshets, and soon a fleet was in movement, straddled by salvoes, a miniature Battle of Jutland, a one-way battle, without retaliation. At least, I thought, it was not the first time a tutor to the family had ended an uninteresting lesson by percussion, only our ammunition was shillets instead of revolver bullets.

For this slight service, I was invited to fish in the saw-mills water, 'for six times', a most generous reward. I went down once, at evening time, but caught nothing. The otters lived in a hollow tree on the bank, and possibly had fished before me, and so all the surviving trout had hidden themselves.

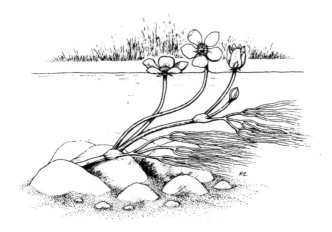

Migration

The Tay salmon fry in the wire-netted outfall leat below Clay Pit had become parr. The blue bars, on 'inky fingers' on their sides were now distinct, their spots more crimson than vermilion from taking the water-flies which floated down to them from the Pit when hatching, or as crawling larvae. There were also yellow sallies which hatched from caterpillars feeding on the leaves of the willow trees shading the Pit.

Soon my little parr would be smolts, eager to migrate down to the sea. I felt a little sad at the prospect: how would they fare without me, and so many enemies in the big and unknown watery world?

Every spring elvers came into the estuary in shoals like drifting ribbon-weed, to make their way up runner and side-stream. I saw a mass of them by the coffer dam of my weir above the Clay Pit. Two and three inches long, they were mud-coloured, flexible and semi-transparent as they wriggled up the wet wood. I watched, lest any get through the screen, fearing for my parr. These eels were the females, they would remain in fresh water for several years, grow-ing into long black fish before dropping down to the estuary in an autumn of their maturity, to swim back to the Sargasso Sea, there to spawn and die. How did they find their way home, across the Atlantic? By nosing into the drag of the tepid Gulf Stream lying on top of, and wandering through the ocean—water tainted by scents of rotting weed, the eels especial smell in memory? They had come that way: did they remember the route, and follow it back to its beginning in the Gulf of Mexico?

One afternoon I discussed this with my old angler acquaintance—he kept everyone at a distance, as was proper for a retired judge, or anyone else for that matter, who did not want to have too many human eels entering the privacy of his thoughts. The judge spent a week every year at The Fisherman's Arms. I had invited him to fish and to dine every year, but he invariably declined, pleading the constrictions of age; but he paid us a visit once a year, at tea-time, and was a favourite with the children.

As we sat in the sitting-room I asked him if anyone had thought of the possibility of salmon finding their way back to the parent river by following the sunken gorge which once, in a prehistoric age, had been the bed of the river, before the continent broke and let in the sea.

'Ah,' he replied, 'I rather fancy that a French writer has suggested that in print already. His theory is that the rivers of Scotland were once tributaries of the Rhine, before the land broke, as you say, and the North Sea was formed. Each river has its old submarine bed; each river-family of salmon feed along that sunken way when they go down to salt water, and return the same way. Occasionally one may lose its way, through greed or shifting currents, and when repletion had stirred its sexual instinct it ascends the nearest fresh-water stream.'

Migration

He helped himself to another patum peperium sandwich.

'But, in general, the fish of each river, members of a particular clan, find their way back to the ancestral river. The instinct to return is in the egg, an inheritance from innumerable generations of salmon.'

'Then each clan is really a sub-species of *salmo salar*, you think, sir?'

'I would not say that I think that. I have read about salmon, I have noted the conclusions of men who know far more of their ways than I do, and until those conclusions are disproved, I shall continue to accept them as possibilities.'

After tea we went down to the Clay Pit, and saw the parr dash down to their feeding places in the screened rillet flowing from the pond. Next May, I said, they would be smolts, and then I proposed to set them free, to go down the river.

'These parr,' he said, 'or those of them that survive the hazards of the sea until maturity, will return to the Tay in due course. Do you intend to mark them?'

I said that I had not thought of it.

'I believe that the usual practice is to pierce the adipose fin, and affix a silver tag there.'

I said I would do it in April, before the parr, which were now in their second year, turned into smolts. From the pond we went into the deer park. The old gentleman watched the Loch Levens being fed, after which we walked up the river, which he had known, and fished, he remarked, many years before.

'But,' he said, 'in those days, there were no weeds here. My goodness, look at them now!'

Half the shallow area of rough water below the Peal Stone Falls was white with blossoms.

'It is much more luxuriant above the falls, Judge.'

When he saw the massed bed of white flowers covering the former mirror-like water, he exclaimed, 'How came the weed to flourish like this?'

I replied that I had planted a few bines some years before, to give holding for nymphs.

'But *ranunculus fluvitans* is surely a chalk-stream weed? The flies of such a stream are different from the flies of a rapid moorland river. Nymphs of native flies live under the stones, and these masses of weed, I see, are already suppressing the stones. And on those stones, moreover, grow algae which is the only food of nymphs in your water.'

I had already felt the awful import of his words, before he went on, 'You have heard of the river Clwyd in Wales, and how Canadian pond weed, introduced there by some-one with the best of good intentions, has ruined all the fisheries upon its banks?'

'Then I have laboured in vain,' I laughed.

'I can only hope,' he chuckled, 'that your labour will not result in harder labour elsewhere.'

This retired judge was a bachelor. Did he enjoy giving punishment to younger men, I wondered, when he went on, 'M'yes. I have been doing some rough calculations. The capital value of the salmon beats to the Junction Pool and beyond to above the tide-head might possibly be assessed at about a hundred and fifty thousand pounds. Still, I must admit it is a very pretty sight, a very pretty sight indeed.' He laughed grimly.' You must write another best-seller!'

Migration

'If I could go to prison, and be allowed to write, it would be my salvation, Judge.'

'Ah,' he said, as he got into his hired motor. 'There is many a true word spoken in jest, my young friend! You must write another *Tarka*. Why not about a salmon this time?'

At night, lying in bed, depression set in. How far had the old chap been joking? The fisheries, exclusive of the netting rights in the estuary, might possibly bring in ten thousand pounds a year to the various riparian owners; and in addition, the rates extorted by the Rural District Councils were half the rents—a further five thousand pounds. These sums at five per centum meant a capital value of *three hundred thousand pounds*, for which I might be sued; with additional costs, since the law must live, the total might well approach four hundred thousand. I remembered the story of the polluted fish farm at Dulverton ... perhaps it was now my turn to be ruined!

At three o'clock in the morning I got out of bed and put on clothes, fishing stockings, waders and brogues; and taking a rake, mattock and scythe from the summerhouse, went forth into the water-dim dawn to begin a task of removing all traces of my weed from the river.

It was not long before I learned why the claws of an otter's front paws were always worn down. Abandoning my steel tools after the first five minutes, I got down to it with my arms and started to pull weed from the river-bed. Soon the sleeves of my coat and shirt were wet; and pausing to straighten my aching back, time after time, with hands resting on lower ribs, my shirt and trousers became wet too. I hauled armfuls of dripping weed, and let them float away with the current, while water ran into my waders and my trousers and socks became saturated. At last, as the sun was rising among the trees, I went home to breakfast, not to rest afterwards with the feeling of good work done, but irritated and careworn; for I had done so little. Back to the river I went.

The two boys, coming home from the village school that afternoon, said that they had seen a man at the sawmills pulling masses of green weed from the water-wheel, while sawing was stopped. The next day they reported lots of weed hung up at the road bridge, and by the three piers of Humpy Bridge. I hurried out, and saw several tons wrapped around the stone cutwaters. The evidence of my guilt was obvious. How could I face the Lord of All, who was down with pleurisy, when he was out and about again?

By midnight I had cleared most of it from the deer park water—except the roots. The next day, walking furtively to the weir, past the little colony of willow titmice, I observed that many long bines were lodged around stones in the shallows. From these, no doubt, new colonies would start. I went on down the river, fascinated by these vegetable pioneers of eventual ruin. Herons and dabchicks would carry the weed to other tributaries of the Taw, perhaps to Torridge, Tavy, Teign, Exe and so on down to the Cornish Camel and possibly, in the course of migration, across to the Continent of Europe. I was done for.

The next day, drawn to the scenes of my crime, I continued on past the Junction Pool, arriving there as the Waterloo express steamed past. I envied the carefree faces staring out of the window. When it had passed I went on down the river, noting colonies of *ranunculus fluvitans* flourishing everywhere. Some were at the stage of the smallest green tassels; others were as large as corn-sacks. It was only a question of time before the entire water-course was choked.

I felt myself to be Tregeagle, that legendary Cornish imbecile who, challenging the gods, had for his arrogance been condemned to undertake two tasks, to follow con-secutively: the first, to empty Dosmaré Pool under Brown Willy on Bodmin Moor, the only implement allowed to him being a limpet shell with a hole in it; and when the tarn was dry, then he must proceed without rest to the sea shores of Lyonesse, and twist all the sand there into ropes. Having purged himself by these works, he was free to spend the rest of his life as he would. That sentence had been pronounced upon Tregeagle in prehistoric times, and the job was still uncompleted. According to a lecturer of the Devonshire Association, of which I was a member (ought I to resign before being kicked out as a vandal?) the unfortunate man had been given immortality at the same time as his sentence, so he was presumably still at it.

To avoid that fate, or its equivalent, I continued my task every morning at dawn. Already my fingers seemed to be becoming webbed, and the thought of ever holding a pen again was instantly rejected. The river was no longer a place of delight, or escape, as it was to herons, dipchicks, kingfishers and otters which once I had thought of as in-truders, and which certainly took no thought for the morrow.

The season of sun passed away; and one November morning we heard that the Lord of All was dead. He would carry home no more bent nails, to be straightened and handed over to his clerk of works. For if a nail was not too worn, it was worth saving for use by one of the estate carpenters: a nail saved for the shoe which saved the horse which saved the rider which brought the message which saved the battle. By devotion to all aspects of his inheritance, which had been impoverished at his succession by death duties and other matters; by his foresight and energy in planting otherwise incult coombes with fir trees—wood saving flesh and blood in due season—the estate had been conserved, and work provided for many whose families had lived off that land for centuries. Did a tenant fall sick? His Lordship had heard of it, and made the matter his concern. He visited labouring men's cottages periodically, to see if all was well: if he saw cream on the table twice in one week, he might ask if it could be afforded. Was there a sick child, needing extra nourishment? He sent cream, or perhaps butter, for the small, shy creature. Was this interference with the liberty of the individual? Those who worked well, who also did their duties in their various ways, did not think so. They knew when rents from land did not support the Big House, in a period when English land had never been so cheap for a century and a half, and it was said in the market place that land was the thing to get out of.

I had told him, one day in the past, about my plan to plant weeds in the river, and he had not objected: but why was I thinking like that? It was my responsibility solely.

You must write another 'Tarka', the judge had said. *Why not about a salmon this time?*
I stood by the Peal Stone Falls in the widening light of a

new year. Under the grey glassy water the tassels of a hundred, a thousand new clumps of *ranunculus fluvitans* were showing. Half the area of the river was now green.

But would a book about a salmon be as interesting to the general reader as *Tarka*?

I worked out that, if it were to sell 20,000 copies before I was made bankrupt on account of judgments going against me in numerous cases of Riparian Owners v. Williamson, I would be able to pay about 4d. in the £.

But seriously, I thought, such a book— The idea took root in my head. I was afraid; it was beyond me; I knew so little; I was disturbed by other matters; the river would be choked, I with it. On the principle that the moment to attack was when one's front was pierced and one's flanks were driven in, I signed a contract with a London publisher, and received a sum of money which would maintain the family for a year, and hardly had I paid it into the bank when a letter came inviting me to visit the Southern States of America. My wife urged me to go, saying that I had worked hard at my desk all the winter.

'But I have been on holiday all the time—apart from writing.'

'Well, I think you have been working. You have been studying the river for years, and talking about little else. I'm sure you'll write a wonderful book about it, once you are away from it.'

'But I don't know how to begin, or what to say!'

'It will come at the proper time. I should go to Georgia, if I were you.'

The disused eel-trap had been secured by a number of old harp-strings twisted together; one of these I removed

Migration

for the silver wire binding the cat-gut. Lengths were cut and inserted through the pennant fins of my salmon parr, then the silver wire was twisted. No labels, no other markings. Having done this, I lifted the end screen and flushed the parr, soon to be smolts, down into the runner.

In the Deep South

The invitation to visit Georgia had come through an American lady in London, who was a member of the English Speaking Union. She explained in her letter that a friend in the South had read an article of mine in *The Atlantic Monthly* about peregrine falcons in Devon, and having a gracious house with only herself and her servants to enjoy it, she had for some years regarded it as a sanctuary for authors where, she hoped, masterpieces would be written.

'Have any masterpieces been written there, ma'am?'

'Not so far,' replied my interviewer, in the softest of Southern voices. 'But you need have no cause for disquiet. From what you tell me of your plans for a new work I would think that there you would find, in the gracious living of the deep South, within the garden of my friend, the very inspiration you are in need of. I do not know if the creeks and rivers there have the particular species of fish in them for your study, but there are several other species, including of course alligators. I do not know,' the slow voice went on, 'I cannot tell, of course, since you have not detailed to me the schedule of your proposed writing, whether such fish as you will find there will be suitable for your study, nor would I be so crude as to ask you to tell me which particular fish you have in mind—' Here the lady paused and looked at me, while I nodded my head slowly, as though deep in thought. 'Wale, I guess that's all,' she concluded, her voice ending in a Northern accent. 'What do you think?'

'I would like very much to go.'

'One more thing I ought tell you,' she said. 'Do not be disquieted when you observe that my friend paints her face.'

I waved the notion aside airily, and took a dish of tea with her, sipping delicately in what I felt was the Southern manner; and when I left the building I had in my pocket two tickets for New York, one being for my return, and a cheque on the Chase Bank for a ticket to Augusta from Pennsylvania station in New York City.

The older forms of Southern hospitality, reminiscent of 'T. E. Lawrence's' descriptions of meals with desert sheikhs, were still, at that time, manifest: thirty or forty guests to dinner, vast silver salvers containing many fragments of chickens, my hostess urging me to fill my plate: legs and wings lifted from her plate to mine as a compliment to the guest on her right hand, and also in solicitude for the thin face of the 'foreigner'.

Later that evening, when the party was over and I was in my room, I turned on the radio. *This is the Atlanta Journal calling, the voice of the South. The Atlanta Journal covers Dixie like the dew*. Every night when I heard that, I felt the tremendous romance of the place. How could I write about a salmon, there?

Dance music followed. It awakened the mocking-bird, that imitator of other birds. Listening through my open door and window, I heard the notes of a thrush—almost an English thrush, with something of the blackbird's quality in its notes, but faster in tempo; then the wistful jangle-cry of the blue jay followed by the throb of the nightingale when it cries *teru teru teru*. Yet there were no nightingales in America. Had it learned the notes from the radio?

Before I was told about the mocking-bird it puzzled me, for it sounded as though several birds were singing on the same bough, all of them hidden in darkness, and one following the other.

It was now the beginning of April, and already people were talking of the coming heat. Every night I tried to write in my bedroom; but it was a mocking-bird life I was leading as I sat, doors and windows open to a semi-tropical moon, my thoughts accompanied by those of a bird which made audible a mixture of other birds' songs; even as, now and then, beyond the azaleas and *magnolia grandiflora*, would arise the singing of homeless Negroes giving voice to nostalgic chants and hopes based on the three-thousand-year-old literary testament of a nomadic Eastern race.

Thus, more or less, passed the time.

I met a most enthusiastic young man with white hair who was paid, he told me, $40,000 for each serial in the *Ladies' Home Journal*. He explained that he had travelled far into Asia to get local colour for his serials.

'H.W. has come here to write his book on a fish,' explained Miss Esmeralda. 'Don't you want to take him with you on your fishing trip, and let him pick up a few de-tails about our Southern wild life?'

In the Deep South

It was arranged that I should meet the author and his wife a few nights later at a bus stop in Valdosta.

'I will have your bags packed ready for your return to England when you come back from Florida, H.W.'

From the coloured butler I had a look that I considered to be one of triumph. But that is another story.

The journey to Florida by Greyhound was an exhilarating experience despite the heat. My seat was just behind the driver, with a cooling stream from the open window. Everything was interesting—the palisade fences made of split boles of trees enclosing fields from the swamp, no posts, but lengths of grey wood laid on top of each other, zigzag for self support.

We thundered at sixty m.p.h. over old narrow wooden bridges and modern concrete causeways across swamps. We watched convict chain-gangs, in their striped clothes, working beside the roads in the hot sun, under the alert eyes of guards wearing big straw hats and carrying rifles at the ready position. We passed avenues of pecan-nuts with their delicate young green leaves—the pecan was a soft-shelled nut which tasted so much nicer than walnut, and with the virtue of the English hazel nut added.

The bus passed several of those carts and buckboards which in Dixie invariably had wheels describing figures of eight on worn and scrupetting axles, as they proceeded very slowly along the streets, drawn by a mule or a horse of such fatigued and emaciated frowsiness as would instantly bring alertness to the eye of any R.S.P.C.A. inspector in England. Old Negroes, in tattered clothes, often bootless, crouched over the reins.

Then into the country of orange groves, while thoughts arose of Delius, who in youth came to Florida to grow oranges—Delius who loved the sun, and dreamed of sun-shine, and those sun-fruits which came from whitest bridal bloom—Delius whose music was love and dream and serenity and impersonal heartache for evanescent beauty in life.

The bus stopped at filling stations for passengers and Coca-Cola. It arrived at Macon at 4 P.M., there was an hour to wait before going on south. I saw lovely girls in that town: every one had grace and beauty. How could I think about a fish, among such mermaids on land? Also, the sandwich bar at the bus station was excited because one of the gang of a famous bandit of that time, Dillinger—who had escaped from prison, holding up guards with a pistol made by himself of wood, carved with a safety-razor blade—had come in on our bus, been recognized and chased, but not caught.

We went on at 5 P.M., with a new driver in a larger bus. He drove quickly, hurling the vehicle about. I read, dozed, drank Coca-Colas, chewed gum, dozed. It grew darker. We passed a truck carrying ten tons of oranges to New York, lying in the roadway, overturned in collision with a 1910 Ford two-seater, looking like half a concertina on wheels; the great big truck knocked out, the slight little old bewildered Ford standing near it. A turtle laid on its back by a cockroach! The driver and I roared with laughter at the comic sight. 'Look at it!' he cried, 'only slightly damaged! Just folded up for a quiet little sleep!' We went on faster than before, swishing past the siren-shrieks of other trucks, carrying red, green and blue lights, which dropped in chromatic whines as they swished by in the darkness.

All this stimulation for less than a cent a mile.

In the Deep South

I met my new friends at the Valdosta bus stop, and there we had supper, before going on to the Hampton Springs Hotel. This sounded expensive; I was down to my last hundred dollars, having refused my hostess's further offer of money. However, all was well, for after a rainy journey, we arrived at a semi-ruinous building standing in a clearing at the edge of a swamp. The hotel was once famous. It had been built for rich Yankees from the North, who in a past age had gone there for a cure by sulphur. Made of wood, the white paint on which was faded grey, it stood in a wilderness of sandy soil, among slash pines charred and maimed by fire. Their gaunt, sad boles arose amidst rusty spikes of palmetto grasses.

It was very quiet in the hotel. The swimming-pool above the creek was deserted, except for snakes. No one drank at the sulphur springs. The place was slowly falling into ruin. I was put in a suite of rooms which only millionaires could have afforded during the fashionable days. The suite, with all meals, cost three dollars a day. I was the only guest in the entire west wing. My two friends and I chewed our food in a vast green-gloomy room; we did not linger there; our footfalls echoed over the unpolished, uneven floor of what was once the ballroom.

My friends went to bed early; I sat, or rather stood up, and sought inspiration by playing a 1909 Edison gramophone, with records a quarter of an inch thick, and scored with such tunes as *Two Little Girls in Blue*.

Walking down the glooms of long corridors I knew by dim whitenesses of eyes and teeth that I was passing one or another of the old coloured women who moved so silently about the place. The hotel was said to be haunted. The atmosphere suited me. I explored. Upstairs in one of the rooms with stained and cracked ceilings there were some old moth-eaten trunks, all that was left of one of the old-time visitors. I imagined that he had come to be cured, feeling, as all adult human beings feel, that in the future he would be a different person; and here he died; and no one knew who he was, or where he came from, so here he was buried. His trunks remained for years; until one day, when he was almost forgotten, they were opened; and what was left was picked over by the Negroes; and now the trunks were empty, lying open on the floor.

In the swamp nearby stood the broken casino, home of goats, snakes and owls, its warping timbers holding what ancient vibrations of love and hope and inner despair?

I found it impossible in such an atmosphere to begin my story of an Atlantic salmon. But at least I had relieved my mind of one perplexity, small as it was. In Augusta I heard a larger edition of the spotted woodpecker drumming—while it was perched on an all-steel telephone pole. It was the same quality of sound: nothing metallic about it.

The sea was seventy-five miles away, but the nearby river receiving my first cast was tidal. Not with salt water running up; the land was flat, the water sluggish, returning upon itself twice every twenty-four hours. Dark brown water moved slowly past the muddy roots of cypress trees, where strange crabs moved from the shadow of the Negro's paddle.

When first seen, these small creatures repelled me slightly: for they had but one claw, monstrously out of proportion to the rest of their bodies. They were mud-coloured, the hue of decay and dissolution.

'Fiddlers,' said my paddler, 'I reckon them's fiddlers right thar, borss.'

I asked how deep was the river.

'Aw, mighty deep, borss. I reckon this ribber is ninety feet deep. Yes sah, yes captin. Ninety feet, boy.'

Later I learnt that it was about thirty feet in the middle.

The boat in which I sat was called a bateau. In build it was between punt and canoe. I sat, a little uneasily, in an old armchair, the broken seat stuffed with sacks, in the fore-part of the bateau. All bateaux were complete only when fitted with broken chairs, for white fishermen. The Negro's front teeth were inlaid with gold—not from necessity, but for the sake of beauty—or tail, as it was called in South Carolina.

Rather a terrifying river for a timid provincial Englishman on his first visit; deep glooms in the creeks; branches of trees hung with moss, a grey lichen which was not truly parasitic, being air-nourished. It straggled thin and dry; but was strong, the suspensory threads within their grey coverings being like brown cotton thread.

Alligators were lying on mudbanks under the trees. Rattlers and deadly moccasin snakes moved in the swamps. I saw a red-headed snake swimming towards us; it dived when my paddler struck idly at it with his paddle. Snapping turtles, their green shells curiously marked in brown, lay by the beds of hogweed, their scaly heads, snake-eyed, poking above the surface.

The act of casting a painted wooden plug for the large-mouthed bass which lay close to the bank by snags and roots was difficult for a beginner. I was unfamiliar with the short steel rod and Pfleuger reel, which tangled the silk line in back-lash: so I watched the birds.

In the Deep South

Small black vultures were sailing far overhead, in the white sky which could only be regarded through smoked glasses. Ospreys, called fish-hawks (so rare in Scotland) were common, gliding and slanting with heads down-held for sight of fish: then the plunge, the *splash!* and the brown and white bird flapping up with mullet or stump-perch in its talons.

One day, in the open river beyond the levees or banks of which lay derelict rice-fields, I saw a white heron. Seeing us, it held its head and beak at an angle of sixty degrees, looking like an unopened slender snowdrop. Then it flew up, followed by its mate, and pitched on the lily pads two hundred yards away. Once these birds were much persecuted, for the 'ospreys' of women in high society.

Across the swamp a crow was cawing repeatedly. Its note was sharper than that of the English crow—a smaller bird, too.

''Coon after its nest, mebbe, yes captin, I reckon that's so, borss,' said my paddler (one dollar fifty cents a day, including information). 'Yes sah. Raised and born on the ribber for twenty-five years, borss. Yes captin, raised and born on dis here ribber, twenty-five years.'

A strange black bird passed overhead, with webbed feet stretching out behind more than its neck and sharp head projected in front. It was like a shaped and streamlined splinter of black glass. It flew swiftly, then glided again, beat wings, glided.

I asked the paddler who, after spitting for luck on the worm he was using as bait, declared, 'No sah, oh no boy, that's a turkey. Yes, captin. Water turkey, I reckon I call that one, borss. I was raised and born,' etc.

.   .   .   .   .

In the Deep South

At night the darkness of the swamp outside the hotel was alive with noises of frogs and crickets: fireflies scintillated, starlike, in sudden turning flashes by the glimmering white walls; the whippoorwill, that large nightjar, cried with startling nearness from a pine branch.

My friend said 'Be careful of snakes; black-diamond, rattler, moccasin. The black-diamond's bite is immediately fatal.' One night, sitting with them in the dining-room, trying to eat grits (maize meal), tough hog, leathery potatoes and pumpkin pie, I saw how funny it all was, so did the black boy who 'cooked', and we began to laugh. I became hysterical with laughter, and fell from the chair. Here was I, under contract to deliver by autumn a book about a Devon salmon, sitting in a ghostly ballroom in Florida, drinking water tasting as though eggs had been boiled hard in it, and then allowed to cool; water which a few years ago was being sold in New York for a dollar the gallon, 'guaranteed for Rheumatism, Indigestion, Dyspepsia, Stomach, Kidney and Bladder Troubles, Gastritis and Skin Diseases'. Scrutinize that quotation; the sulphur water was guaranteed for those ailments. Guaranteed to give you them? Or to rid you of them? *Order to-day at our risk* said the old prospectus. The water could be bought in five-gallon demijohns for four dollars. The creek outside was full of it. I lay on the floor, laughing.

That night, sitting on my bed and typing, the windows open for the heat, I heard footfalls padding about. It was an effort to continue sitting there with the door unlocked. My spine felt icy cold; the hair at the base of my neck stood up. To test myself, I opened the door and walked slowly down the corridor, avoiding the places where dry-rot had removed some of the boards. I trod in darkness and

In the Deep South

silence, feeling my nervous energy sparking like fireflies out of my body; and walking as in a dream beyond fear, I thought myself to be of intense sunlight, and therefore intangible by any forces of evil. I walked down the passage, and back again, my hair bristling and fists clenched against —what? Those strange fluttering footfalls? Perhaps the convict from the chain-gang who got away three days ago? My nerve gave way when I touched the door-handle, and pushing with my shoulder, I ran into the room, slammed the door and turned the key.

Mosquitoes whined just outside the wire-gauzes. The great-barred owl uttered its startling bubble-hoot. Surely the place was haunted. There were stories of Negroes being burned alive in the old days. Furniture was moved about at night. I confess that I felt some security with the door locked, sitting on my bed and typing my impressions, while the whippoorwill cried loudly just outside the window, and the fireflies flashed.

The river was horrible and mysterious. I saw a snake roll into the water and lie at the muddy edge coiled up in a tight figure of eight, only its head out. Touched by the wooden paddle, it uncoiled, loosening a frog which immediately stood up, hands over head, and dived away. It was a piteous sight suddenly become very funny. While I was laughing some wild goats and hogs—oddly together— came down to drink. The hogs—the 'peach-fed ham of the South'—had a habit of stamping on snakes and eating them.

There were panthers in the swamps, which were full of deer. Fish leapt before the underwater rush of alligators; the 'gators revealed only by a rash of mud-bubbles arising.

I had to say to myself, This is Florida, this is where

the youthful Delius dreamed and planted his orange groves.

That night a storm of lightning played in the east, like gunfire over Le Transloy Ridge, fireflies crackling-flashing, high aerial shrapnel. *Whippoorwill! Whippoorwill!* echoing among the pine trees of the swamp, where in the afternoon, riding back on a pre-war Ford drawing the boat on a trailer, I saw convicts of the chain-gang working.

Was the escaped stick-up bandit hiding in our derelict wooden palace, with its weed-grown gardens and creepers over windows? As I went along the dark corridors to dinner of grits and leather hog-flesh in the decayed ballroom with my two friends, whose room was eighty yards away from mine, I thought that the poor fellow should be warned against eating the food, and drinking the sulphur water.

One morning when Edison and I were going fishing for big-mouthed bass in one of the rivers near the Okefinokee Swamp we stopped at a filling station for gasoline, and the inevitable Coca-Cola. Every filling station—even the little one-man shacks in the wilderness—kept a supply on ice of bottles of this brown aerated liquid, drunk out of the bottle. We were having our five cents' worth when there was a clattering rattle on the road outside, and an auto with four Negroes in it came to a standstill. That well-worn cliché 'came to a standstill' is an apt description of what happened. It didn't pull up; the driver didn't stop it. Looking out of the wooden store behind the gasoline fillers, we saw an ancient battered rusty car with burst and faded hood, flapping bonnet and flat tyres tied to crenellated rims with what looked like the remains of several pairs of obsolescent trousers. Apparently the car had no brakes, but it had some gears, which operated through a loose and wobbling prop-shaft, and thus somehow, with ignition switched off, and pistons, connecting rods, main-shaft, clutch, gear-wheels all protesting against motion, it came to a standstill.

It was very hot that day although it was only early May, and I did not take much notice of this particular outfit; but returning some hours later and seeing it at the same stand-still outside the station, the occupants still sitting motion-less under the gaping hood, in the same order and postures, I asked the proprietor about them. He said they had no gasoline and no money, and as it was hot and they had some food, they weren't bothering. Some time, some-how, they would get to Miami, their destination several hundred miles south.

Edison and I were driven many miles over sandy tracks by coloured men—paddlers or guides—after fish. One of our guides, tall and dignified, drove his Ford V8 very fast over sandy tracks and over wooden bridges—*bump—crash —bang!*—with a sure hand, and a high-pitched laugh when-ever we were thrown into the air. I feared for the springs but needlessly. The auto had been built for such country. It was new, and well kept. The driver fished as surely as he drove, casting his wooden plugs for bass—called trout in that part of Florida—as far as forty yards across the water, with a four-foot steel rod, while standing under tall cypress trees and having less than a square yard of space through which to throw his lure. Like most Negroes, he was deeply humorous and content, laughing at what to others might seem trivial incidents—he was a great child. He and I laughed at the same sort of jokes. When we were worm-fishing in a shady bend at the river for red-bellies, and a catfish or a mudfish took the bait—recognized by the way they bored deeply and slowly on the bottom of the river —he chuckled and laughed. 'Another old catfish, I reckon!' he chuckled and squeaked, showing his white teeth and enjoying the joke: for these fish were solemn, scared, sluggish-looking creatures, and their appearance amused him.

I enjoyed being with the Negroes; deep contentment flowed from them into myself. There were four of us in the party—two white men and two paddlers. We caught no bass; it was the spawning time, as I learned at the end of the trip, and fish wouldn't strike, or rise as we said in England, when they were laying their eggs. But it was good to be out on the water with such companions.

Our coloured guide took us about fifty miles a day, and his charge was only five dollars each—including lunch. In the evening, when we were packing up, my friend offered him a drink of corn whisky, which he carried in a giant thermos flask; but the Negro refused politely, saying he never drank when driving a car. As he already drove over tracks that made the going almost like motion on a bronco, I was glad to hear this. We saw turtles on the track, and once a rattlesnake was wrapped round our near fore-wheel.

Why did this country of sand, palmetto grass, thin pines slashed for their life-sap, to become turpentine, pale grey sky, pale grey sand once drowned by the sea which mur-mured among the shallows of the Gulf of Mexico—why did this land give a persistent feeling of vacancy, of some-thing lost under the sky, a haunting silence in the midst of

In the Deep South

the sunshine? Since all feeling for Nature came from within I knew that it was of myself, an exile in a strange land, one whose deeper thoughts were always of England.

Yet there was, apart from myself, a vacancy in the sunshine. Day after day, as I sat in the light of the high silver-burning sun, wearing only shoes, cotton trousers and dark glasses, writing not the salmon book but an autobiography while the small and concentrated shadow of a cabbage palm moved so slowly towards my chair, I found myself suspending all thought and hope in order to listen with the mind's ear. There seemed to be a remote pain, a sense of loss, in the very air.

For days I had been travelling on concrete roads and sandy tracks to rivers, lakes and creeks, our wheels pressing a way through thousands of square miles of flat, sandy land. Everywhere the same sight: league upon league of rusty palmetto grass, often burnt; a few poor slashed pines standing thin, and seldom straight, against a sky bleached of all colour.

Sometimes our car passed through areas of scrub growing as though hesitantly among the stumps of great trees. Only the stumps, grey and crumbling; never any great trees. The earth we traversed was almost as open as the sky.

I asked Edison as we were eating lunch by a creek if he felt anything vague, strange, melancholy, about the country. He was a world traveller in search of big game, a rich and popular writer, unlike myself; one whom I secretly envied, as he appeared to be, while yet remaining sensitive, a wholly happy man. Was this feeling, I asked my American friend, merely an emanation from my slashed and melancholy self? To my relieved surprise he replied that he always felt the sunshine of Northern Florida held the ghosts of great trees which were 'brutally logged off' during the last century.

'Some of the species are now extinct,' he said. 'The lumber kings got concessions for next to nothing from the Government, and they went through the whole country, clearing everything away, big timber and small stuff, treating the forests as the bison were treated, not giving a damn so long as they got the dollars, Henry.'

'Yes, Edison, I feel that this country still bears the wounds and death feelings of those trees. You may think it strange, but I feel myself that the tree spirits, or the Tree Spirit, were so shocked and wounded by the clearing that they or It just ceased to be. I have wondered if it is merely my anthropomorphical identification with the trees, or transposing effect and cause, that I feel distress in the unending bleakness of this sandy country, the decaying stumps, the weak scrub growing up as though it knew it didn't have any real right to the open sky.'

'You are right, Henry. It was so cruel, so damned senseless, the way they logged off everything. . . . And I kind of feel that even now, when we are begininng to think of afforestation and planning things in a way that will be good for every *thing*, if you understand, as well as for every man, well . . . perhaps we'll be forgiven, and trees will grow again down here once more.'

'All Things Linkéd Are . . .'

My visit was over, it was time to leave for the North. I was excited, all the current of my being set towards the East. Also I was down to my last fifty dollars. I had my return ticket; but the next boat from New York was in four days' time. I knew my money would not last, so decided to sail at once from Montreal.

The South already held memories. I felt sad that the life of so many scenes had already passed away. There was the little cracker boy who paddled us one day, clad in the usual blue jeans, barefoot, and he could neither read nor write, but was so polite and naturally a gentleman; the hanging moss in the cedar swamps; the misty blue eyes of the old 'poor white' in the woods who hired us his boat—he shaking and poisoned by home-made corn whisky.

There was the forest creek on the banks of which I had been sitting for days in solitude, writing, not alas, the salmon book, when suddenly a hundred girls and boys from the school in the neighbouring sawmills town appeared, and the swimming bath behind the hotel was alive with cries and colour and splashing laughter. There was a yellow-haired girl in a red skirt whose passion was the stars, and whose dream was to be an astronomer, she told me while the mandoline played and I felt myself to be sixteen again. And the teacher, in charge of the class, seeing me writing there, seemed to feel an importance about it that no one else had felt. She came to me and said, 'May I tell my class?' Then she said, 'Boys and girls, here is an English writer, Lord Williamson.' They cooed around me, curious and gentle, the girl in the red skirt seemingly inspired, because she had spoken to the author first.

Another picture, of a rattlesnake swimming across the river, holding its tail out of water, to keep the buttons, which made the rattle, dry. And the white light of the sky, the high silver blaze of sun, the white egrets fishing by the riverside—the nesting females no longer slain for partial reappearance on the heads of women in a previous age of jewels and feathers. And so much else to remember—the Negro morality play staged in the Negro church, with the Devil in red, an attractive Devil with his capers, grins, winks and offers of whiskey, lipstick and children's toys, to tempt to destruction the heaven-bound souls of all ages. The success of the play was assured by roars of happiest laughter! And that white preacher who came to the town and took seventy-five hundred dollars away after a week's exhortation—some of it over the local radio in this manner, 'Friends and brethren, the Lord has spoken, the Lord has awakened one of us into the Light—my friends, at this moment Mr. Richard Lowry is praying for guidance whether he shall send for the Lord a cheque for fifteen hundred dollars, the sum doo for my life assurance, which I have not, as I have taken no thought for the morrow, but have got goodness organized for this Drive against Sin— hold it folks!—a telephone message just received at this broadcasting stoodio, saying Mr. Richard A. Lowry is mailing that cheque right now—the Lord has answered his prayer—Hallelujah, Hallelujah.' The preacher, whose name was Ham, cleaned up over $7,500 during his week in Augusta.

All night the train rolled north. At sunrise I looked through the window, half expecting the landscape to be English, since I was now in Canada. At last I was in Montreal station, watching for and claiming luggage: a dash into the street to buy a bottle of Canadian rye whisky, from a government store served by an official behind a wire grill. I wanted this in case I was ill on the crossing, as I had been all the time coming over. Then coffee and toast and marmalade in a cafeteria, and back to the luggage guarded by a redcap and into the bus and down to the docks, and up the gangway and down to C deck aft and a little cabin over a propeller. I had one dollar fifty cents left.

As a hope and duty to acquire equipoise before reaching Belle Isle Strait I walked the decks with determination that there should be no *mal-de-mer* this time. Quebec, with the Château Frontenac on the heights, dropped astern. Dark blue were the mountains against the northern twilight gleaming on the widening sea-way. I felt very cold after the South, and my greatcoat was in a trunk in the hold. The *Montcalm* passed into the open Atlantic south of Cape Race, and ran into fog. Icebergs were beginning to drift south. The air was bleak, inhuman. Rise and fall and rattle, creak and uninteresting sameness of everything conquered me. Through the porthole, with what relief did I see the last pale sightless peak in the grey heaving sea! We were beyond the drift of icebergs; and on the way home! When I recovered from my fear, and was up once more,

I began to enjoy myself. In the company of some young men from various Canadian universities, travelling steerage for adventure and economy, I trespassed on the select decks and saloons forward, telling each other our experiences, theirs seeming so real and substantial, such as crossing the Atlantic on cattle boats, driving sledges with teams of huskies in Greenland, while they fed the dogs on frozen salmon, and endured blizzards: while mine were only rearing fish from eggs in a runner at the bottom of the garden, digging out wasp-nests and feeding them to trout while standing on a bridge over a small West Country stream; watching herons, otters and spawning fish; listening to river sounds changing with the atmosphere at evening and in the night.

'How's about a turn round the boat deck, fellers?'

Round we went again, laughing and talking. Then there was silence, and stillness.

What was that light on the port bow? The Bishop Light? Could it be? We all ran to the rails. There, far away over the sea, shone the first light of England!

I had given the unopened bottle of rye to the steward in lieu of cash; but I did a wise thing on my return; I opened one of my two bottles of dry champagne, kept in the tiny cupboard under the stairs, and drank most of it, the children having some out of egg-cups. This wine, followed by fried gammon of bacon with eggs, put heart into the wanderer returned, so that the fitting together of the rods, to place them in their rack on the landing above the cellar, with the net hung beside them, and enamelled lines turned from reels to winders, was a shared family affair.

'Dad, all your fish are all right! I fed them every day!'

'I helped too!'

'Yes, the little boys and I went together. I do hope you will find everything all right.'

'How's the weed?'

'Oh, it looks all right. The river is still running high. They say the springs broke again, we had so much rain when you were away.'

'Dad, there's lot of salmons in the river now!'

'Yes, I took the boys down to Steep Weir, the fish-pass was open. We didn't see any there, but we did at the saw-mills.'

Soon I was back in the habit of walking beside the river, as though I had never been away. One morning I saw a heron by the bridge, and realized that it was the beginning of the annual visitation by young birds cast off by their parents. Among the younger birds I caught sight of the familiar hollow grey wings gliding down to the pool below the Peal Stone Falls. By the bleached greyness of the wings and thin body I recognized Old Nog, who had been fishing my river for at least six years. He recognized me at once, and the downward glide changed to a slow oaring of faded wings as he flew on in a leisurely manner to his next fishing place up the river.

On that place, a mossy rock below an alder tree, the heron wheeled and glided and changed his mind once more. He knew that the weather was wrong for trout fishing. The air was suddenly cold, and near to frost; no flies had hatched that morning; no trout were poised in any of the runs, waiting to feed.

The water after the high spates of early spring was very clear, the gravel beds were all shifted and scoured clean. The river, and the weed beds, looked quite new. The pale amber hue of peat and marsh water from the Exmoor hills had all run away into the sea. The water had a bluish tint, very cold and clear, the spirit of salmon.

Old Nog knew that the trout were under the mossy stones and reddish roots of alder, waiting for warmer airs and a hatch of flies. So after wheeling once again he beat slowly up the valley and alighted in a rushy ditch by the railway viaduct, and, after looking around for possible enemies, which meant me, he put down his head and began to peer into the ditch. Then he took slow and stilted steps along the course of the field drain.

I walked slowly up the valley beside the river, peering for salmon. Glancing at the heron, now three hundred yards distant, I saw the thin white line of its narrow head and beak as it watched me. The long neck and body were hidden by the rushy bank of the drain.

As I went on up the river, the heron continued his slow and stilted walk along the ditch. About a hundred yards from where he was peering there was an old oak tree. When the trunk was between me and the bird, I changed direction and moved quickly towards the ditch, keeping the trunk between us. I reached the tree without being seen by the bird.

It had, however, missed me. Anxiously it raised its head and stared towards the river bank. Apparently it had a sense of the continuity of time, for it got out of the ditch and spent the next five minutes waiting for my reappearance. I lay on the grass and watched it round the base of the tree.

It was cold lying there, so I got up and walked casually towards the ditch, pretending I hadn't seen him. He got down into the ditch in order to conceal his body, and began to walk up the ditch. I wandered on, making my mind a blank, lest he feel my intentions.

There was little wind in the valley. Casually I strolled on. Old Nog, scrambling out of the ditch, began to walk faster over the boggy ground, which inclined upwards to the edge of the larch plantation on the hillside. I got to within about sixty yards of him. Why didn't he fly away, I wondered. This shyest and most suspicious of elderly birds usually rose when I was a quarter of a mile distant. Then it occurred to me that he could not take-off uphill. If he wanted to fly, he must turn round and run towards me, to get air under his wings.

I walked on the faster. Old Nog took longer strides. Uphill he stalked. By an open gate leading into the larch plantation he hesitated. I was now thirty yards away, well within gunshot of my quarry. I stopped. Old Nog hesitated, then walked into the wood. I went on. He now had no alternative but to continue to walk up the path, or between the rows of trees. I walked faster. So did Old Nog.

He began to look wildly about him. 'Kaa-ck!' he cried, then walked on. I ran after him. I got to within five yards. He turned and pointed his beak at me. With trembling hands I loaded, cursing myself for not having done so in the house. Then, holding the Rolleiflex and trying to focus I saw the bird running towards me with wings outheld. 'Kack! Kaaa-ck!' he screamed. I clicked the shutter, and then turned, scared by that sharp beak which any moment might pierce one of my eyes with a snake stroke. Had I not once found a sea-trout of four pounds in weight after a freshet lying in an eddy with a hole in its head as big as my thumb, and its side torn open for the eggs within? And in olden time, how many peregrine falcons had been

killed by a heron borne to earth by the weight of a cast of
hawks binding to it, to defend itself within a shield of
wings, lancing yellow spear as its enemies?

A sweeping draught passed over my head with a grating
curse, and a sort of fishy stew was dropped upon me.
Hollow grey wings were wafting away smaller and
smaller. But what a photograph it would be, I said to
myself, quite unique! the exposure had been 1/100" with
the largest stop: there was plenty of light, the film was a
fast one. I watched Old Nog flying up the valley in a
leisurely manner to his next fishing place, and then
examined the camera to verify stop, shutter-speed and distance of focus. Yes, it would be sharp in detail! Heron
attacking man! Surely it would have considerable news
value? Where should I send it? It was a scoop. *Author
Routed by Old Nog!* Then I wondered if in my excitement
I had forgotten to remove the guard of the lens? So it
turned out; instead of a menacing beak and pale eye, I had
taken a photograph of the back of the lens-guard.

Next morning sunlight coming through the wide-open
casement window above the stairs gleamed on the var-
nished rods standing against the cream-distempered wall.
The sun was now entering the constellation of Taurus; it
was the time of the annual festival of the smolts. I sat in
my writing room, pen in hand, white paper before me. A
book has a beginning, a middle and an end. It must have a
curve like the Sun in space, as seen from the earth. First
the Sun mounts upon its orbit, brings wider illumination
to all life. Then as the Sun reaches to the heights, it stays a
while in glory, before descending to the west, where,
among clouds hanging upon the earth it has enlivened, it

reveals its colours through the vapours of the upper airs; and one more day is ended when it sets below the rim of ocean. Then darkness is to the earth; and the nightingale, which has migrated by the pattern of stars, sings to the night; while the river glows with fluorescent hues as seen by the eyes of fish, the rocks may be dark red, a white flower of crow's-foot shines blue. Constellations underwater glitter with colours; every thing has its spirit; all things have life, even the dead. I could feel these presences, of the elements that composed me; but they would not take form. Shaken by feeling, I moved about the room, knowing that I must wait for the influence of truth.

Outside the open window I saw the lodge-keeper's ducks busy in the Clay Pit. It did not matter. My parr were now in silver coats. Perhaps by now, carried by the grey rush of the river, they were in salt water; or passing down The String between the Two Rivers, where the ebb tides jostled, and the bass, spiny of gill and tail-fin, were taking them.

In my shadowed room, as the sun crossed above the plantation on the hill to the south, the luminous quality of the air beyond the casement made a shut-in existence unbearable. Looking out to the lawn below I saw, beyond the dark yew's shade, a small delicate globe of light arising slowly, followed by another, and a third. The olive duns were drifting over the garden from the river. Water gushed everywhere below the moor, feeding the river's many runners. There was no colour in the water, in the sense of suspended matter. It was clear as bottle glass, faintly green.

A gossamer gleamed across the window space, shine slipping along its length as the wind carried it. I could remain indoors no longer. Taking my nine-feet split-cane rod from the rack, I put a brown gut leader in its damping box, and with rod and net went to the river.

Looking over the parapet of Humpy Bridge, I saw dull greenish-silver flashes as a salmon below turned on its side to take nymphs. Beyond the alders fringing the west bank five horses were rolling and kicking on the grass. High in the wandering airs rooks and daws soared and plunged, crying and sporting. From the trees came the laugh-like yaffle of the green woodpecker, and the cooing of wild doves. I walked down from the bridge, while the horses sprang up and galloped away across the park.

My rod felt very long, after the short steel American rod with which I had cast, in vain, for bass in the rivers of the South. It also seemed to be very fragile. If I hooked a big salmon in that water, and it went downstream, I would lose it at once. My line, with backing, was under a hundred yards in length. And even if the fish didn't go downstream, how could I play it on such slender tackle, with water-weight added to its own? How manipulate the rod past all the bankside trees?

I had been told, in Scotland a year or two before, that a salmon worked always against the hook. Therefore, in heavy water, one should turn the head of a fish going downstream by letting the line drift in a loop below it, so that, feeling the water-drag, it turned upstream again. I remembered this as, with a feeling that I was at last going to get a salmon in the river, I threaded the line through the bronze snake-rings, and the agate ring at the top.

The gut leader was the strongest I had, the one used in the burn at Islay, slightly frayed when it had been rubbed by the fish boring down to the rocky bottom. I chose

another moth-eaten fly, name unknown. Most of its peacock herl body was eaten away. It was a small fly, the hook
being, like the others in the case, japanned black, with a
round bend about the size of my little finger-nail. A ragged,
thin, rakish ruin of a fly, quite unlike those seen in the
tackle-makers' windows of St. James's Street and Pall Mall.
I tied this relic of Victorian days to the gut with a figure-
of-eight knot, and hurried away along the timber-wagon
track beside the river. An overwhelming impulse pos-
sessed me to take a clean-run fish.

First I fished the Fireplay, having crossed the river by
the footbridge below the viaduct. No rise there, and none
in the Wheel Pool immediately below it. So I recrossed
the footbridge, and went down past the oak at the bend
below the Wheel, past obstructing alders, and coming to
the water-slide, fished the deeps there. Not even a trout
gave me a pull.

Below, the river widened into a fast and shallow stickle,
which slowed into the Alder Pool. Just below the clump of
alder roots was a ledge of rock, and beside this ledge was a
gorge where sometimes I had seen a stale summer fish
lying after a freshet. This was the bit of the river that
resembled the straight stretch in the Islay burn, where I
had hooked my first grilse.

It was the best lodge for a fish in my water, being in the
middle of the length straightened during the eighteenth
century. I began to feel excited, as I remembered that afternoon beside the burn, its black water moving at the same
rate as this glass-hued water before me, and with the same
lazy surface swirls into which, at the end of a straight line,
I had dropped the Black Dog atop the flow, to strike the
surface with the faintest flick, without splash, without the

'All Things Linkéd Are . . .'

least drag, like a large insect on the surface. Strangely, it was the same occasion, returned in Time.

I was tense and expectant as when I had knelt in the heather, and known in a remote way that I would get a fish. I had known it faintly, but not believed it, since one can believe only something that is before one, that has happened. The other *knowing* is more tenuous than a drifting gossamer, because it is neither seen nor has it happened. And now, beside the Alder Pool, I had the same feeling of prescience as I half-knelt upon the grass, to send my line back and fore, almost languorously; and then, shooting the line straight, with a final loop released, my vagabond fly at the end of its flight dropped lightly upon the surface—*flick*. I lowered the rod point, letting the fly go down almost as fast as the current, for a foot or so. And just as I had known, but dared not believe, as I raised the rod point I felt a weight on the line: not much, but the line was held: and with a thrill of the never-to-be suddenly achieved, I lifted the rod with firm wrist and felt a considerable weight there as the unseen fish, turning away, drove home the barb. Then as it leapt out of the water and I saw its size I stood up and looked round for the children, to shout to them that I was into a salmon, that I wanted the big net standing in the hall!

The fish leapt again, blue and white and silver, and shook itself so that I feared it would break the gut, and then it was rushing past me upstream and the reel was screeching—a dozen pounds of compact muscle in silver armour, and my rod weighed six ounces and the gut would break at two pounds, perhaps less with its frayed end.

The line caught in the roots of one of the many alders growing on the bank. I felt it scrape. Wildly I pushed the

rod in front of me, crashing through brambles and nettles
to free the gut. Fortunately at that moment the fish
returned, and began boring, to get to the bottom of the
rock ledge, and rub the hook from its jaw. I put on a strain,
all I dared, holding the butt back. The rod curved; the
fish leapt; I expected it to shake itself off, but no, it leapt
again, shaking its head. Then I remembered to lower the
rod point; and it was off downstream, the reel whirring
as all the tapered line was taken off, then the backing, a
coarse line attached to the end of the enamelled line. If it
ran out I knew I would have to go into the water, otherwise the trees and bushes on the bank would foul the line,
and the weight of the fish, going with the current, would
break me. So into the river I walked, glad I was not in my
waders; even so, I must be careful not to slip over. In my
nailed shoes I felt my way, almost gliding, as the water
took me smoothly downstream. The bottom was uneven, sometimes gravel and then a rocky pit through
which I floundered to my chest, with a feeling of really
living.

Above the fall the current slowed, and the fish with it.
My line went over the waterfall, the drag sent the fish up-
river, it passed me, now in the weed-bed, as I stood there;
and seeing my legs, a few feet in front of it, it turned, to
rush down again, but to turn once more at the falls. I eased
the line, hoping it would swim up again; but once more it
rushed off when it saw me. This time it zigzagged into a
weed-bed. I wound in line, and holding the rod over my
shoulder, tried to push the fish out with my foot. It went
off upriver for the third time, turned again and went downstream, taking out all the line, so that again I was flounder-
ing after it, in water half-way up my thighs, my feet en-

tangled in bines of weed, yet managing to drop the rod point, and ready to let go the rod if the fish went over the falls.

The fish went over, but I held to my rod as I toboganned over the sill, going down on my feet, and with water gushing over all of me but my head, waded forward to follow the extended line under the tree-trunk bridge which crossed the river there. I was now in rapid, jabbling water, and more sure of my footholds. I leapt downstream after my line, thinking that surely the fish would break me in the shallows, with so many big stones in the bed to catch the gut; but to my surprise I saw its back fin out of water as it lay close in to the broken-grassy bank. I got below it, wound in my line, and walked slowly up to it. It shot away across the stream, but came back: this time I stood still as I reeled in, having passed the rod to my left hand, to hold it high and keep slight pressure on the fish's mouth.

Slowly, very slowly, I leaned down and gripped the fish by the wrist, the small part below the vent, keeping my thumb towards the square tail. It shook violently, but I held it, and lifted it on to the grass, as my children approached, shouting to each other that Dad had got a salmon.

The fish was clean-run, porcelain-white underneath. Around the vent were blood-marks where sea-lice had sucked between the scales. One louse still clung there; the fish was twenty-four hours in from the sea. I stared at it, marvelling at the thick shoulders, the flanks of silver and azure, the fins of pale coral. There were purple-brown spots on its gill-covers: the same spots it had worn during its first two years in the river, before going down to the

'All Things Linkéd Are . . .'

Atlantic. I wanted to put it back in the water, to leave it to the life within it; and while I thought that it should live I sought to find a smooth clean stone, with which to strike it a blow on the head; and picking up a stone, stood there between the two ideas or impulses; then kneeling, I took its life.

In the past I had sometimes returned from trouting, carrying a basket filled with stones, to be greeted with, 'Not a salmon, at last?' by my wife playing up to the old joke. This time the catch was too large for any basket, so I carried it home by a tattered red silk handkerchief tied to tail and jaw—a curved ingot of silver. It drew down the marker on the spring balance to eleven pounds.

Soon the dreamy azure was gone, with the faint coral tinge of its fins, all the spirit of its ocean god vanished from it, as it lay on a dish in the larder.

I managed to write the first few chapters of the book, by self-discipline, every word forced against my reluctance. There was no life, for me, in the descriptions of rock, wave and fish. In such a mood as Conrad, who made with words the greatest sea-pictures in English literature, must have known, I left my desk one evening, while the sun was still high in the south-west, and set forth with my smallest trout rod, to walk up the river now dropping back to its early summer level, and showing white in many places where blossoms of crow's-foot covered its surface. I walked slowly, in my heavy brogues and waders, to the viaduct, and passed under its honey'd scents on my way to fish for trout in the pool at the bend above.

Cumbered as I was, it was burdensome to scramble through brambles and alders to the waterside. I did not want to fish, but pulling out the line, unhooked the hackled fly from its ring above the cork handle; and having greased it lightly, I got up and stood at the edge of the water, to stare with dull eyes at the grey and blue and brown stones of the gravel under the clear water, at the moss on the rocks, at the star-clusters of wild garlic growing on the banks amidst hart's-tongue ferns, at the pale blue water-violets, the celandines and the lilac milkmaids.

The leaves of the oak, massive at the bend, were a tender green, but a few weeks out of bud. I saw all these things in a glance: I had seen them many times; there was no stimulation in seeing them now. Feeling that my life was wasting away, I moved up to the dark pool, comparing myself, to my disadvantage, with the natural oak, which had been growing there hundreds of years before I was born, and yet was comparatively younger, renewing itself every spring with the uprising of sap from its roots.

While I stood there, a unit of the higher civilized consciousness almost entirely isolated from the flow of life around it, my eye caught a pale drift of movement amidst the oak leaves. It was a mayfly, about to come down to drop her eggs on the water—the final act of her life.

Now mayflies were not common in the rivers that ran down from the moors of the West Country. The rivers ran fast, scouring rock and gravel, disturbing the fine sand mixed with silt wherein the larva of the mayfly must burrow and feed and be concealed during the two years of its watery life. This silt lay only in the eddies and backwaters, where the main force of a river in spate was retarded by water-drag, or backwash, and the push of water against water caused comparative stillness. There the silt settled;

and as more water arrived with earth washed by rain from the cultivated fields, so more silt was dropped there.

In my two miles of water there were only about a dozen places where the tiny grubs, hatching from eggs, could find sanctuary. Therefore in the river I was beginning to know, mayflies were uncommon, if not rare. I had watched one trout behind another moving away from a spent mayfly floating downstream—scared of the big, unfamiliar object.

As I regarded this mayfly, I thought how she had hatched from the water, after two years in cold darkness as a burrowing grub, towards noon of that day. As I observed her fluttering climbs and pauses, her falls and sudden side-ways dippings—lightly to touch and rest on the water while dropping her egg-clusters from the three long whisks of her tail—I began to marvel anew at the mystery and fidelity of the life- or spirit-cycle of which she, frail beauty, was but a servant. After two years in darkness, instinct had led her to the opaque light-sheen of the river-bed, which before she had dreaded. The grey nymph, about an inch long and shrimp-like, had then crawled up the stem of a flag-lily growing under the bank; the pellicle of the swimming nymph had split, and a pale winged creature came forth into the strange element of shining air; and after moving her short, damp wings, shaking out the creases and feeling them growing strong in the sunlight, found herself moving upwards into the warmth and free-dom of paradise.

Slowly the new world of trees, grass, clouds, blue-flicker-ing runs and ripples, and sun-pointed bubbles, was defined within the new sense of sight. Though she beat her yellow-green wings so rapidly, she rose up slowly, drifting with the light water-breeze of the early summer morning, until before her she saw, suddenly, the dark branch of an oak, and there she clung, curve of body upheld in balance by her wings, veined and fragile, and the delicate sweep of paired whisks. There she rested and dreamed, needing neither food nor drink, ethereal body awaiting its destiny in the decline and fall of the sun.

I had watched male mayflies, called drakes, in the evening by Humpy Bridge, black and white creatures rising and falling, with almost inaudible clicking or whirring of wings, beside a grey pillar. Perhaps the stone of the parapet, warmed during the day and retaining its heat in the evening, caused an uptrend there as cooler airs filled the valley; there the drakes, the few that had survived into young summer, were wont to gather, during the brief hours of their lives in air. The most I had seen together were seven. The drakes rose and fell in a winged fountain as they awaited the females, and the climax of their day of light and joy—the mating in the height of the sky: followed, inevitably, by the falling apart—disillusion and death for the drakes; transfiguration for the females.

With enlarged and shining eyes, her wings now divinely blue as the very air of heaven, my mayfly flew down to the river, and waited beside an oak leaf while all her life gathered within her and became defined in one purpose— to seek herself in the river that shone with the sky. Watching her as I stood there, I wondered if she knew why she must seek the shining water: probably not; it was the Spirit which moved her. And watching the rising and falling, the pausing and side-slipping, the least touch and rest on the surface, my spirit cast its cumbering pellicle, and I lived anew. With wonder, with gentleness, with compassion, I watched her as she seemed to rest upon the water, while the stream bore her away—then she was rising again.

Slow and tremulous had been that first flight at noon; but now towards sunset the mayfly was experienced in her approach, beating her wings together to rise, now suddenly shifting with alternate wing-thrusts and slanting down (as though to deceive a watching fish) to the water, to release her eggs.

I felt my eyes to be clear again, as a child's; and I heard again the cry of the water, the mingled sounds of bubbles breaking, the swirl by dark-green water-moss, the white racing between the rocks, the lap of the dark eddy under the oak roots by the bank yonder. I saw the startling and wonderful green of the ferns, the clear colour of the petals of the water-violet. I do not exaggerate this, it is no literary emotion, no heightening afterwards to make a pretty piece of writing. So clear was the water, so beautiful with its pellucid flow over the multi-coloured stones of the gravel, each with its minute stir of gravel-speck and sand-whirl— the entire river-bed was alive, in movement—the clear water flowing from the rock of the moor, our earth, our home: the beginning and the end: our mother.

So it was for the mayfly. She was tiring; she fluttered with less certainty; she was hesitant; she seemed now to be afraid of the river. The sun was sinking below the tops of the spruces which grew in mass up the hillside to the sky. Then I heard the song of a chaffinch, that gay bird whose nest is so beautifully shaped and moulded of moss, horsehair, lichen and feathers. But O, how the song jarred, how coarse and reptilian it seemed, superimposed upon the tranquil river-noises of sunset attending the dance of my mayfly into the stream of eternity. For I had watched, in the noon of the previous day, a chaffinch waiting in an alder above the bridge, to fly out as a mayfly rose from the river, to snap it in its beak, to return upon its perch to await the next, and the next, until it had taken the entire hatch of the year from the eddy by the bend where the horses came to drink and cool their legs.

I turned away; I looked back again. Death and transfiguration—or transfiguration and death: which was the order? I can testify that the mayfly, nearly spent, was changing swiftly from azure blue to pink, the hue of sunset. She had but a few more moments of life. I wanted the river to take her away, her wings dispread, her head in the water that was her first, and her last, friend. As the finch flew towards her again I turned my head, and wound in the line, and fixed the sneck of the hook in the little ring above the cork handle of the rod. With a last look from the bank I saw the chaffinch sitting on a hazel branch, preening itself before giving song again; and below, riding rapidly away in the race at the pool's end, the pale speck of the mayfly.

In high summer the river was beautiful with white blossoms of the water-crow's foot upon the gravel. I learned, as I had learned before, that the ideas of inexperienced men often work by opposites. Thus the greatest patches of weed collected the most silt, making shoals in the shallows; and when the river-level dropped in hot weather, the shoals became islets. The exposed weed on these islets died away; and between the islets the currents ran faster, undercutting the new gravel banks. Fish lurked there, in water made the more lively by its swiftness. And mayflies, which were scarce in the river owing to the few silt beds in which the larvae could burrow, began to increase. The trout in other years, when I was gone, would feed on them, and grow bigger. I would not be there to see them, for my work on the river was ended. When the corn harvest of that year was being carted, my salmon book was finished, and when another Michaelmas came I gave notice to leave the fishing cottage, and the river.

The book had not been easy to begin, to sustain and to bring to its end. Does the swallow arrive, otherwise than through peril, and will-power, to the north where its young must be raised? Does not the salmon face death when it ventures into shallow waters, the nurseries of its young? Is not the mayfly, most aetherial of creatures, born but to die; and in dying give back what it has held, for a while, in trust for others of its kind? That is what the river taught me anew; for it seems that fallible man must learn, again and again, the eternal truths by which alone he can find salvation from the perils of the mind.

Trutta the sea-trout, the old pug, who drove through the net in the estuary, and later drove an otter, as I witnessed, from the spawning redds above the Fireplay, and bumped it in the Wheel pool, again and again, until the otter left the water; Salar the salmon, Gralaks the grilse, Danica the mayfly, Libellula the dragon-fly hatching on the bark of the alder, below the nesting hole of the lesser spotted wood-pecker—they lived in or beside the river and I saw them, and when the time came I gave form to my impressions in the book.

My work in the valley was done. For the last time I fed the fish from Humpy Bridge, and climbed the alder by the Fireplay. This tree had borne me during six years in its upper branches, and had felt the wounding foot-thuds as

'All Things Linkéd Are . . .'

I went up and down again. Alders are sensitive, soft-wood trees. It is the fate of some alders to live near water, and to lose the last of their sap by fire; for the wood grows in straight grain, and makes the best charcoal for drawing, giving beauty to men by its death.

My observation alder died during the last year of my tenancy. Whether it grew weary of the blows of my feet I do not know, but when I left, fungus in pale yellow rosettes which also fastened on salmon weakened by prolonged months in the river, was growing upon the tree.

When autumn came and we were packing up to go to Norfolk, where I had bought a derelict farm in order to reclaim it, I went down to the swamp, to take one last look at the Clay Pit, before pulling up the wooden dam in the runner, by which water was led off into the pond. It had been a wet year, and the springs were still gushing. There was a fair flow of water at the bottom of the garden, on its way to join the river just below the road bridge. When I looked into the pit I stopped still: for there was a salmon, its tail moving slightly in the quiet flow of water past its length.

I crept nearer, on hands and knees, moving as slowly as I could; and raising my head beside a clump of half-withered cock's-foot grass I saw a twist of silver wire upon its adipose fin.

So it had come back to its home! Individual memory, and not racial instinct, had brought it to the pond in which it had been reared to smolthood, which it had known as its protector, its mother; and to which it had returned, now that spawning was imminent.

I turned it down the runner, through which it fled in

'All Things Linkéd Are . . .'

violent fear of shallow water to the river; and I broke
down the weir, releasing the little spring-fed rillet upon its
old course. Then I returned to the cottage, and lit the fire
in the hearth, and sat before it, playing Delius's *Song Before
Sunrise* on the gramophone, knowing that I had come to
the end of another seven-year cycle of my living.

April–September 1957
Devon.